MEDITATION FOR EVERYDAY LIVING

Second Edition, Revised and Enlarged

Michele Meiche

This book is dedicated to all who read it, apply its
principles, and make these meditations their own.

I thank you for having the courage to live your own life
authentically and to connect with your own true nature.

You truly are an integral part of making this
world a better place.

Thank you for giving me the honor of sharing
my gifts, experience and knowledge.

Blessings in Light,
Michele

Acknowledgments

To God/ Spirit/All That Is for imbuing me with gifts of intuition, and spiritual connection that I can share with others allowing me to be a channel for spirituality, creativity, inspiration and upliftment.

To Spirit for flashing down the idea to my funnel of light.

To spirit, my guides and higher self for always being there for me.

I wish to thank for unwavering support, honesty and belief in my work and life path: Diane Lerner, my soul sis and Rachel Jeanne, Thank you for your insight and belief in me, and for at times seeing more in me than I could see in myself. To Mojgan for her belief in me, and more importantly what I am blessed to have come through me; and for her being a reflection of truth and wisdom. To finding the flow in laughter, crowded city streets and snow. To Jennifer Kelly-Matthieiu for connecting me more fully to my creativity and believing in the vision and "The Work", and for being a wonderful collaborative partner. Thanks to Paolo for being a visionary of light. To Pierrre for his amazing gift of photography.

To Josie Kelly, both student and teacher, for walking her talk and sharing her gift of being a quiet spot with others.

To Dina Wolff for feeling I had information worth sharing, trusting me and believing in my work, and for being there as a friend.

To Caryn Ward for her assistance and support.

To Rev. Cheryl Ward for seeing potential and opening a door, and for Rev. Michael Beckwith for being a constant source of inspiration, awareness and the reminder that we are all Divine Expressions of the Light.

Lori Bregman for her courage on her path, trust in me and sharing the wisdom with others. To Kristen Kosinski for being an instrument for spirit. To Susan Arthur, my assistant who always helped with the details and Cleo. To Cleo for teaching unconditioned love. To Yoshi a being of abundant love and joy and to my brother Chris for just "being there on the journey."

To all my teachers and mentors, especially Beverly Martin of the Marian Assoc. in England, Doña Chuey Jésus, and Dr. Dee Hahn for instruction, guidance and an integral part of my foundation. To Colin Campbell on the other side who saw my light and gave me a chance. To my mom una espiritualista y maestra on a bumpy road. And a heartfelt thank you to my loving grandpa Henry. To my dad for his words "Honey, you can do anything you want. I think you can."

For *all* my clients, my students who are also my teachers.

For all who have helped me grow, shine and reflect back the truth of their love and beauty.

To all who read this book apply its principles and make these meditations their own. I thank you for having the courage to live your life authentically and connect with your inner nature. You truly are an integral part of making the world a better place.

Thank you for giving me the honor of sharing my gifts, experience, and knowledge.

Blessings in light.
Michele

Foreword

"Meditation is paying un-distractible attention to Reality."
- Reverend Dr. Michael Bernard Beckwith

This little book is packed with powerful tools and techniques for entering into the meditative state. As Dr. Beckwith's quote reminds us, meditation is a state of being in which one's full attention is given over, and surrendered completely, to Absolute Reality. Students hoping to meditate often struggle with the numerous distractions offered by the external world of effects, and with the endless stream thoughts that flow through the conscious mind.

How do I stop my thoughts? How do I relax? How do I become calm and peaceful? Am I doing it right? These are essentially the questions that beginning students have once embarking upon a meditation practice. This little book lives up to its title, *Meditation for Everyday Living*, in way that is easy to follow and simple to understand. More importantly, this powerful little book is like a guide on the side, who everyday assists the student in further developing their meditative practice.   It can be used by the person new to meditation as well as the person who has been meditating for years. Michele Meiché gives simple and clear instructions, through numerous breath work exercises, for working with physical relaxation techniques. These exercises assist the student to better understand that achieving a meditate state is really a *process*.

The book is filled with meditative processes beautifully described. The dynamic imagery of the descriptions serves to assist the student in understanding how to achieve a state of physical, emotional, and mental surrender.

This is an excellent book with a variety of everyday techniques and exercises to meet every kind of challenge and achieve a level of mental calm, surrender and relaxation.

I highly recommend this book to the student of Truth who seeks to deepen his/her meditative practice. It will take the student from noticing his/her thoughts to actualizing the infinite potential within.

The beautiful way in which meditative processes are presented allows the student to have an intimate tryst with the Omniscient, Indwelling Presence, thereby achieving an un-distractible attention to the One Reality.

Reverend Cheryl J. Ward, J.D.
Dean
University of Transformational Leadership at Agape
Agape International Spiritual Center, Inc. Culver City, CA

Table of Contents

Second Edition Preface

Written summer 2007
in a small beach cottage on the west coast.

The first edition of this book was really created as a "How To" and "Handbook" for my varied clients.

This second edition is keeping in alignment with this; however, I have added additional information and processes to facilitate a deepening spiritually.

The past few years I have been teaching more and really seeing what supports a path of self-development and spiritual integration. The two focuses go hand and hand and you really can't have one without the other. You learn so much about yourself and life when you begin to meditate.

Many of my students embark on this path and have profound changes in life and attitude. They may have started out for stress reduction, medical reasons, to stimulate their creative mind or because it is now a "cool trend". And, lo and behold they begin to really breathe in, to really take in life, for this is what the breath in really symbolizes.

They also begin to really breathe out, to really let go: for this is what is symbolized by the out breath. This allows them to find their own inner rhythm, their own right timing thus allowing them to relax into their life, trusting themselves and their life path more and more.

In the I Ching it is said, "Have an acceptance of fate and be open to being guided." This to me is spirit led living. It is living in the meditative state.

We may not always be able to change our fate. We may not like what the vicissitudes of life bring to us, however we can make our movements through the terrain of our life path with an inner connectedness, inner knowing, peace and calm.

Meditation is a tool and aid for this. Through a consistent use of mediation as a tool of self development and an access point to go deeper into ones true nature one can live in this state every day.

There is an ordinary perfection to all of life. There is a magical, mystical wonder to us as spiritual beings in this life experience. We are both human and divine, mystical and practical. We are Spiritual and Material. When we awaken to the truth of this and live this awareness in a balance that supports our true nature we are enlightened.

Meditation is the tool, the door way, the breath is key, it is the carrier.

The meditative state is the way in which you want to travel on your life path.

It is a lighter and more fulfilling way to travel.

I hope this book brings more joy, inner peace and awareness on your path. May it make your trip a more interesting one.

Blessings
Michele

Introduction -
How to Use This Book

The Path is the Goal one way is through the practice of meditation.

Although a man may be book learned, if he does not apply in his behavior what he knows, he is as a blind man, who even with a lamp in his hand cannot see the road. From the "Stanza 169 of the "Shes-rab sdong-bu" (Tree of Wisdom) of Nagarjuna (ca 100BC) translation 1955 by Professor Chen Chi Chang...

The best way to use this book is to *use* this book!!! Really, as with any new skill, art form, activity, talent or anything we are learning practice makes perfect. And remember meditation is a practice that then becomes a state as you practice it consistently... More on this in the chapter Meditation defined redefined and demystified. These guided meditations are inner process to assist you in your self- development and spiritual integration. Each of the guided meditations is to assist you on your path and spiritual unfoldment. Each meditation has a focus and a purpose that you can use to enhance your everyday living. Whether for healing, stress reduction, letting go and moving forward in your life, connecting to your inner knowing or for a deepening of your spiritual connection these meditations are a tool that can be integrated daily or as need be. The guided meditations will make your spiritual awareness and practice more concrete because of the systematic nature of the processes. Meditation is about life and living. It is with this awareness that the chapters in this book are structured to give a good firm foundation of information, technique, structure and instruction that one can personalize and use in their everyday living. Much of what is covered is what one encounters on their life path; whether a long time meditator, yogini, yogi, student or teacher. Hopefully, you will see that the teacher is the student that becomes the teacher that further studies and learns to again be the student.

In the words of the Zen parable- Before enlightenment chop wood carry water. After enlightenment chop wood carry water.

We all walk the same steps; the steps of our path, with enlightened living the steps are just a bit lighter. ☺

I invite you to use this book as a help aid, source of support and a 'how to manual'. Use this book when you really need to and during the times you simply want to unwind or do a little escape.

You can ear mark the pages, highlight the meditations that you feel are pertinent to your life and even make post it's of the portions that you feel most apply to you. You can keep a copy at home, at the office and carry this book in your coat, your breast pocket, purse or backpack. You can also keep a copy in the glove compartment of your car to use while waiting in traffic or while traveling by car.

You can use this book in the back of a cab, on the train, on the subway, or even in the grocery store or post office line. You can use this book to prepare for upcoming situations and decisions.

You can also use this book when you begin to feel stressed out or anxious.

My editor mentioned she hated being put on hold and waiting on the phone. Who doesn't? It seems like such a waste of time, she said this would be an excellent time to use this book. I couldn't agree more. These are the times that we need to easily access the meditative state.

The structure of this book is based on the traditional meditation technique of repetition. These meditations are basic, and yet an experienced meditator can use these techniques to deepen their practice and as tools for alignment of oneness.

The meditations in this book use the same basic structure, so that you really learn them and they become second nature. Repetition allows for a deepening of your practice and for the breathwork and meditations to become second nature for you. This repetition allows the meditations to become second nature to you allowing you to personalize them to you as you see fit in your practice.

It is similar to playing scales on a piano The "scales" don't get more complicated or varied; however how you *"play the scales"* get better and better and how you play the pieces of music get better and more individualized. So that you have a musical style that is your own. In this way it is said that music and musician are one.

It is also similar to a professional dancer. One practices "bar work", as in ballet or does "routines". But, a dancer doesn't stay at this point; a dancer learns the routines and choreographed dance pieces until they become second nature. In fact there is a point for a dancer when they see certain movements they know what is coming next... They are so aligned they sense and tune into the next movement. At this point the dance and dancer are one...

For a consistent meditator there is a point where one's meditation practice becomes a meditative state of being and awareness that is more and more lived, and more and more easily tuned into, aligned to and allowed. I use the words more and more, because a consistent meditation practice builds to the meditative state bit by bit. For this reason it is important to be more "process" oriented rather than "result" oriented as you integrate meditation into your life.

Going for results is an over emphasis of the ego mind or "little self"/"lower self" In meditation you are accessing or aligning to the "higher self", the more expanded aspect of you. The place of inner knowing, intuitive awareness, the place of oneness where you know all is ok and you are safe, secure and right where you need to be in your life. This not only brings relaxation and peace of mind, but also allows you to access the part of you that actually knows and believes this. This is the part of you that has come up with creative solutions in the past. This is the part of you that has turned challenges into growth. This is the part of you that even if at the 11th hour, has made stumbling blocks into stepping-stones for better living. Unfortunately the "little you" forgets this. Mediation is a tool for your ego mind to remember this. This way you can harness the energy and focus of the ego mind and use it more positively and healthily.

The main suggestion I have for you is to just use this book. Use the technique of repetition to focus on the doingness of practicing meditation. This will allow you to go deeper and not scatter your energy, focus and dilute the natural and organic outcome of your meditative practice. If you practice this way you will get to your goal. You will more and more easily attain the peace, calm and inner knowing you want.

The meditations are short so that you will use them daily and *throughout* the day. There is no kudos for meditating for 20-60 minutes twice a day and not living in a meditative state; or not using your meditation techniques to counterbalance a stressful situation. In some ways it is true use it or lose it.

I have seen in my practice over the years many chronically angry yogis. Yes, they meditated daily, did their yoga, didn't eat meat, wore only organic cotton and all white, yet they were awful to be around. We are all meant to practice what we learn and become more self-aware.

Meditation is coming off the mat and out of the lotus position. It is time to live this state of being and awareness.

The way the meditations in this book are structured the guess work is taken out. You have the foundational techniques to build upon. It is like lifting weights. If every day you lift a 5lb weight eventually you will build muscle and lifting that weight will begin to feel easier and easier until one day it feels light. So light that you may up your weight. Or perhaps you just notice you could up your weight. You just observe this and witness this. Some of you may up your meditation time by sitting longer formalized meditation; some of you may up your meditation time by living more and more in a meditative state. Either way it is ok. It is your practice and you need to individualize it if you want it to become a long-term practice for you that you use.

Make the meditations your own so that as you practice meditation the meditative state can then become your habitual state of mind for your everyday living.

"Meditation is an exercise that puts you in a more calm, less stressed state of mind. Meditation allows you to remove your inner critic, and focus on the here and now without letting your mind wander in destructive directions. "- Michele Meiché from Vegetarian Times article

Meditation as Awareness

In the Buddhist Sutra it is said:

To realize your true nature, you must wait for the right moment and the right conditions. When the time comes, you are awakened as if from a dream. You understand that what you have found is your own and doesn't come from anywhere outside.

Meditation is a form of awareness. In this awareness there is no rushing, no striving, no pushing. There is timing, a flow. This timing and flow comes from within, from the Tao, or way. You notice in the Buddhist Sutra it says, "You must wait for the right moment and the right conditions." This is called Divine Right Timing, or Right Timing. It is beyond our little mind to know this timing. We arrive at this timing, and in this timing we are always on time. This is the timing that gets us to a meeting "on time" even if we are running late. We get there only to find there was a memo for a time change, or the CEO is 15 minutes late, so we are there before they are. How would we know this logically? We wouldn't. This is the timing that has us 5 minutes late and we miss a car accident. Does this mean we leave all to "chance" and release our responsibilities to "be on time" or complete our obligations? No, it does mean we cultivate a mind set and life that allows for a more expanded awareness to come in and be integrated into our lives.

To meditate, to be a yogi, practitioner of yoga or meditation; or to live in a meditative state does *not* mean to be without feeling or emotion. Many beginners along the spiritual path or those that want a reason to not deal with their emotions many times have this belief or agenda. The supreme gift of meditation is the understanding on an intellectual and feeling level that one is perfect as one is. Yes, perfect… Perhaps one's actions at times are less than perfect, or one is going through hard times. Yet, when the meditative state is achieved on a full times level one see the Divine play of life. That one is where one needs to be and is suppose to be in their life path, and that their life has meaning and is integral to a universal structure. A person can be sad, angry or bored; however one now knows and feels that they are not their experiences. A realized being has the awareness that he/she is thinking thoughts, feeling feelings; yet there is a part of oneself that is timeless, perfect and unchanging. When we live and act from the "meditative state" we are in an expanded state of consciousness. We are accessing our higher mind, the one beyond duality, and the part of our mind that is intuitive and yet balanced with our logic mind.

A realized being realizes that he or she has the experience of emotions; but is not of them. One can experience the emotion of anger; yet a part remains calm and centered. There is a releasing of judgment, blame, preoccupation with fear, and most of all a lessening of the comparison of one's life path.

This realization reduces a lot of stress. So much of the stress we all experience is because we are watching others in their life and wishing we had what they had because someone how we have been led to believe that they have more, are happier, or have a better life.

The grass is greener on the other side adage.

Which as a therapist I can tell you is just not true. I hear the stories of many lives, whether celebrities, musicians, students, politicians, executives, successful stock traders millionaire, billionaires, or someone making $15,000 a year each individual is glancing sideways supposing that the person next to them someone has it better. When in reality we all are pretty amazing. Each of us a divine reflection perfect in our individuality. We are like a snowflake from the same source; yet each individual design unique in its own beauty. We each arrive on earth, and like the snowflake no two snowflakes float down the path to earth in exactly the same way.

A meditation practice is a journey, just like your life path. You are on this journey, and a part of you has some ideas, good ideas. This part is the ego mind or "little mind", some call the local mind. There is another part of you that has some even better ideas. These ideas are not yet as well known to you. This part of you is your "higher mind". You can't get to the better ideas by having the "little mind" drive the car on this journey. A misnomer many have about meditation is that you become "zombie" like or that you give up your ego, or that your "ego" is "bad". This is so far from true meditation; or being in the meditative state. Meditation is used to become more aware, not to "check out" or avoid issues. Meditation is not an escape it is a route to life not a way out from life.

The ego becomes a true and authentic reflection of you. Through meditation and living in a meditative state there is less fear and so the will of the ego mind is sublimated to the higher mind and expanded consciousness. Some call this Divine Mind, Collective Unconscious, The Colletive, All That Is, Higher Self, God, Spirit, Soul Centered, Alla, Atman, or Buddha Nature. What you call this and how you access or tune into this state is up to you.

Another way to look at the practice of meditation is to liken it to a transmission of a signal. You are accessing, aligning to or tuning into this signal. The better you are tuned in, the better the music sounds…the clearer the sound.

A signal that has a lot of interference, especially a wireless signal makes a lot of static noise and picks up other input from other sources. It is like tuning in a station on a receiver. If the station isn't well tuned in you don't hear the station as well, or you hear two stations overlapping, or, you can even hear some discordant sounds.

Our mind is like this. We are receivers. Some people' life force and therefore mind are weak with dis-stress and dis-ease because of a weak signal or lack of alignment to the higher mind and expanded consciousness. It is really difficult to feel relaxed and healthy if you are receiving too much input from the lower mind, such as fear, negativity, lack consciousness, limiting beliefs; or too much static from conflicting input and sensory overload.

On this journey one must have an idea of where they want to go, and yet be open to enjoying the scenery. In meditation you are allowing yourself to become more receptive. This requires a moving beyond the ego mind, and yet integrates the ego mind. The ego mind becomes submissive to the higher mind or higher consciousness.

In traditional meditation teachings a meditation teacher or guru would give the student a meditation that was specific to the person's mind and mental, emotional state as well as spiritual development. Traditionally meditation, similar to a hatha yoga practice was taught individually to suite the student's specific needs. As individual beings we are all similar, but not the same. Our minds are a bit different.

Some of us are more mentally based, some more emotionally and some more physically focused.

Traditionally a meditation practice would start with a session of hatha yoga asanas (physic al postures) specific to the "type of mind" a person has. After one would perform the specific asanas then one would "sit in meditation". This is also known as a formal meditation practice. Perhaps a person working through a lot of fear would be given standing postures for grounding and stabilization. Or, they could be give forward bends to bring the heart (anahata in Sanskrit-seat of the soul, place of inner knowing, higher mind) above the head (place of intellect & ego mind)

A good meditation teacher will take this into account and construct a practice that balances out the individual's mind and body to create alignment, attunement and harmony, to create a union —a union like in the practice of yoga. Yoga means union. Through your meditation practice you are creating a healthy union and bond of body, mind, spirit and soul.

Meditation Defined, Redefined
and Demystified

You are surrounded by a wall of thought. It is so easy to come out of it. You don't even have to dig a hole in the wall; you don't even have to open a door. You have simply to stand silently and see whether the wall really exists or only appears to. -Osho

Meditation is an inner process using the mind to go beyond the mind. Meditation allows one to see beyond one's thoughts and surface pulling. The thoughts that go round and round our mind and the surface pulling of the push and pull of everyday living is an illusion. This does not mean that we don't' experience it, and that it is not "real". Yes, we all experience the "hectic" schedule, the push and pull of responsibilities and the twist and turns of life. However there is an awareness and state of being even more real. There is a calm and flow in between or beyond the thoughts and there can be peace in the middle of a chaotic day.

Meditation is also a technique or practice to calm and center the body-mind.

Meditation is a practice in that you practice "it" and at a certain point you begin to live in this state of being.

In using the state of meditation you connect with your inner awareness and the detached or neutral observer. In this state you observe, watch with love, self -acceptance and compassion.

In this state one realizes that they have a mind and a body, yet are not just the mind or the body. One begins to recognize and know that one is not their thoughts, their feelings or emotions yet expresses and experiences life through thoughts, emotions and feelings.

There are many techniques of meditation. Many of these techniques are based and used by certain religious principles.

Every religion has a form of meditation; yet the actual name may be different depending on the belief system of the religion. However, meditation is not religious in and by itself. Meditation is a practice to then learn how to live in a meditative state. Meditation is the tool; however living in a meditative state is the goal or outcome. A soft goal to create the environment to allow this state to be aligned to or emerge.

(My definition)

The Webster's dictionary has defined meditation as: "a deep contemplation, continued thought, as reflection. Solemn reflection on sacred matters as a devotional act."

Ken Dychtwald in his book Bodymind, an established classic in this field has this to say on meditation: For me meditation is simply a word. It is a word that describes a particular mood or state of consciousness that your bodymind (body and mind which in meditation you focus on the reality of this union. MM) enters at certain times throughout your life. This mood or feeling state usually occurs when you are totally selflessly involved in an activity to the point that there is little or no separation between you and what you are doing."

Some spiritual teachers and practitioners state that meditation is a technique that deals with transcendent state of awareness, upper levels if you will. They then go on to state that it is an aspect of yoga (which means union or yoke) A union and awareness of the body and mind, or of the spiritual and material.

In studying many religions and philosophies they all seem to have a couple tenants in common- "Do unto others as you would have others do unto you" and some form of meditation, contemplation, or prayer.

Some religions call meditation contemplation and are uncomfortable with the term meditation. Some doctors are comfortable with the term visualization or guided imagery. And, in many schools you can teach guided imagery and stretching for relaxation, but not meditation and yoga. Some people are comfortable with self hypnosis or medical, but not the term meditation as for some one term conjures up mental images of a eastern mystic with a turban with fears of indoctrination and the other reminds them of a process they control coming from a 'certified and perhaps in their mind validate healthcare professional.

Well, on some level it is *all* the same- just different terms. I am comfortable with all terms as I feel they suit as many individuals as there are terms. And, these terms are changing and being updated over time. The way we express our spirituality is a continuum. Over time the ways will change as our needs, wants and focus changes. There was a time that only business execs used a computer, now most households have them and use them consistently. We may change the form or the version of our spiritual practices or meditation; yet there will always be some basics that remain to build from.

I am hoping to share with you some building blocks that you can then individualize and make more your own. You can study a lot of different forms or techniques and decide which form or term is right for you; or perhaps you will create your own perfectly suited for you.

The venerable Chogyam Trungpa in his masterpiece book 'Cutting Through Spiritual Materialism' quotes a saying in the Tibetan scriptures: "knowledge must be burned, hammered and beaten like pure gold. Then one can wear it as an ornament." So when you receive spiritual instruction from the hands of another, you do not take it uncritically, but you burn it, you hammer it, you beat it, until the bright, dignified color of gold appears. Then you craft it into an ornament, whatever design you like, and you put it on. Therefore, *dharma* (spiritual life practices) is applicable to every age, to every person; it has a living quality. It is not enough to imitate your master or *guru* (teacher); you are not trying to become a replica of your teacher. The teachings are an individual personal experience, right down to the present holder of the doctrine."

For me the doctrine has to be molded to the times and the guru is within. A teacher is a way shower. And those that are shown a way then show others the way, until we each find our own way together. There are many ways. You will know what way is right for you by how you feel on a deep level. If there is a quiet calm and a peace about 'your' way and decisions then I would bet you found the appropriate way for you.

I am a teacher who continues to learn and to pass along what I learn.

I realize that the guru is in you... No one knows more about you than you. I am simply here to assist you to connect more fully with all aspects of you to live with more peace, love and fulfillment.

Remember, your spirituality is naturally inherent. It is inside you. It is a natural component of who you are. You can use many terms to define it, or redefine it in contemporary terms. You cannot 'not' be spiritual. You may not be aware of this component of your nature; yet it will call out to be heard, acknowledged and spoken to. For some it starts through poetry, through dance, through music, or perhaps through a surfer surfing the waves or a hiker hiking a mountain trail. Your spirituality is a good friend who never leaves you. And like any long time good relationship their needs to be a lot of time, care, and energy put into it. If you put the time, energy, focus and love there you have a friend for life. A friend you can always count on and even feel in times of need or joy.

The practice of meditation is a form, or way of tending to this inner nature. Meditation is simply that- a practice. As you practice the form of meditation it becomes a part of how you view the world and the attitude in which you experience the world. You therefore naturally feel more peaceful, calm; and your life is in a flow state where you experience your life as synchronistic. There may be challenges; however you have the tools to meet those challenges with a calm state. The tool of meditation is to be used proactively daily and as needed. Meditation does not mean there is an absence of issues or concerns. It means that you feel a foundation of peace in your day to day living and interactions.

"In silence, stillness, and solitude the beauty of all is revealed. I see this revealing in a crowded street, a walk a long a desolate beach, in the eyes of a child, the wrinkled hand of an old man.

This silence, stillness and solitude are present in the conflict of war, and the dissonance of miscommunication. There resides this peaceful still point if I but awaken, feel and see it so."- Michele Meiché 9/03

Typically meditation unless obviously stated is done with your eyes closed; however there are open eye meditations, as well as walking meditation practices. Remember, eventually you will be aligning and accessing this "meditative state" more and more consistently and living from this state of being, so it won't matter if you are walking, driving, talking, negotiating, tuning within for inner guidance, problem solving or relaxing. As you do the meditations in this book, you will be more easily able to access this state of being at will, again this is the point of a meditation practice- to live in this state, and make decisions accessing your inner knowing from this state of being.

Since this book is a beginning of a meditation practice, or perhaps a renewal; I suggest you experiment with your eyes open and closed unless one option is expressly stated. I still use these mediations and I have been meditating for over 20yrs.

In the practice of meditation it is best done in the beginning with your eyes closed. One reason that this is done is to put a focus on our inner state, since we humans are so externally focused. Also, on a physiological level we greatly minimize external stimulus and distraction by closing our eyes. I would at least have some part of your meditation practice with your eyes closed in silence, stillness and solitude. You can use music or sounds to assist in your inward focus. Research has shown that music of a certain cadence and rhythm greatly enhances meditation and relaxation. I would suggest music without words that is instrumental and between 74-78 bpm. There is a lot of wonderful meditation, massage and healing music now available that is easily accessible. Meditation is a tool to bring you back into peace and balance. This tool is not to only be used in quiet, peaceful surroundings; but to also be used to attain a meditative state no matter where you are and what you are going through.

The main point is to make your meditation practice time a sacred and special time for you; whether 5min., 10 min 20 min or an hour. Frequency throughout the day is definitely better. The more frequently you access this meditative state your mind and body will become more familiar with it and will have a healthy craving for this state, much like physical exercise or eating healthier foods. This healthy craving will create a beneficial habit where you take your spiritual and meditation practice more and more into your everyday life.

Setting Your Intention

Confucius said "Study without meditation is labor wasted; meditation without study is perilous."

Remember, my example of the "chronically angry man"?

Well he was not studying. He was *just* meditating.

Meditation is not enough. It is a part of our life and spiritual practice; however not the only focus. We must study.

Yes, books are good, classes too. However, we must learn to study us. Yes, ourselves. We must learn to watch, observe and know ourselves inside and out.

We must come to know what we really need and want. Not our friends, our family, society, but what we really need and want from deep within our core.

To do this we must connect in and begin to have a love, tenderness and mercy toward our growth and our errors. We must have self-compassion for how we can err or just change our minds and want to do "it"; whatever it is differently. And, we must learn to do this with self-love, self-understanding and compassion. If we can't have compassion and understanding for ourselves how can we for others? We can't.

True compassion comes from self -understanding and Self -understanding comes from respect.

If I respect myself I take the time to know myself, my needs, want and motives.

If I respect myself I honor my desires and interests and I set aside the time for them.

When one has self respect and self love one is essentially saying "I deserve to live my life" "It is ok that I have these interests" "It is ok I have these thoughts and feelings, likes and dislikes." "It is all ok, as long as I am not hurting myself and others, It is ok I self express in this unique way." "This makes me-me" You get it now? You have to be ok to be you, to claim your right to be.

And, one way you do this is by setting an intention or intentions in all you do <u>and</u> setting aside time, energy and focus for your intention. You need to see yourself and your life as sacred and important to focus on.

Your intention is what you are intending. What are your motivations? Why are you reading this book? What's your motive secret or known for reading this book? How do you want it to assist you on your life path? What would you like to handle, to heal? What would you like more awareness in?

This is your *intention*

Your *attention* is the way you incorporate your intention into your life. It is the time spent. It is focusing on your intention. It is the activities that further enhance and support your intention. Your attention is and out picturing of your intention.

An intention without thought to the ways you will put your attention on your intention sets you up for failure and not being able to follow through on your plan.

Many people have great intentions, but don't put the supports in their life to reinforce their intentions.

When you set your intention and incorporate ways to focus your attention on your intention you are now *engaged*.

You are now vested. You might even be a little excited or inspired, maybe even hopeful with this whole idea of meditation.

Setting intentions actives us from the inside. We are no longer doing something from a rote point of view. We have a use, a purpose and the plan is how we focus and use our attention.

For some their intention may be spiritual, for others health-wellness, for some inner knowing, others accessing higher mind for problem solving… The uses for a practice of meditation and accessing the meditative state and living in this state are numerous. There are too many ways to mention here. The ways are as individual as we all are unique.

Take time for yourself and get in a more relaxed state or meditative state where you can contemplate.

This is known as contemplative meditation.

1. Ask yourself "How does meditation and this journey of self discovery, learning and growth fit into your everyday living?

   What is your intention with meditation and a meditation practice?

2. Ask you how will I and can I give attention to my meditation practice? "How can I use my medita-

tion practice? How can I be more in a meditative state?

How can I spend time on my intention?

What situations in my life can benefit by meditation?

What ways can I incorporate meditation into my life?

Note your answers in your meditation journal.

Use this as a guideline for your meditation practice in a flexible way.

Your intentions and ways you put attention to your intentions can and will alter and change over time.

Progressed Relaxation

This is a process for relaxation of the body and calming the mind.

My intention for putting this in the book is for you to become very aware of when your muscles are tense or relaxed. Many clients of mine would exclaim, "I am relaxing"! Yet, when I would look at them I would clearly see that their breath as shallow and quick and their shoulders would be slightly raised.

Many times I hear people ask "How do you relax or how do you know you are relaxed". We know we are relaxed in the beginning by knowing when we are not relaxed.

I am sure you have had the experience of driving and feeling tightness in the neck and shoulders. I have learned over the years that this occurs because most of us (I use to do this years ago) drive with our shoulders slightly raise and a little forward.

Over time our muscles develop a memory and voila the shoulders stay in this upraised position. This memory can be undone, with awareness and relaxation and deep breathing.

So keep a check on your driving posture, and for that matter your posture in general. Your posture; which is how you hold yourself in the world can indicate how you are doing internally, from and "inner state" point of view. Your posture can induce a lot of stress or alleviate it. This is one reason why if at all possible having the spinal column aligned by keeping the back straight, not stiff, is stressed in a meditation practice. There are some asanas (meditation postures/poses) that you let the head slightly bend forward with the gentle weight of the head. In saying this best and most enlightened posture is the inner posture. This is an analogy for our "inner state." One can be doing "all the right" postures, breaths and meditations on the outside, and still have a roaming, scattered mind and fidgety body. Inner posture is key. And key to a clear, aligned and peaceful inner state is an awareness and acceptance of what is.

This doesn't always mean we "like" what is. It does mean we accept and don't try to rush to our future or linger with a longing for our past.

This cause a discontent that worries our mind erodes our fortitude and diminishes our hope and inspiration for life.

Meditation is a good cure for this by bringing us into the present moment to find an appreciation and understanding through the awareness of "What Is"

An integral part of meditation is noticing. The more one notices the more aware one becomes. This in itself is a form of meditation.

So, begin to notice how you are feeling, and what you are thinking…

And bring your attention and focus back to your breath.

◌ჳ
Progressed Relaxation Meditation

Allow yourself to lie down in a comfortable relaxed position.

Close your eyes.

Focus your inner vision on the heart-lung area of your body and just notice your breath.

Notice how you are breathing.

Notice how you are feeling.

Focus on your feet and toes. Tighten your feet and toes for a count of 3 and notice how they feel tight.

Now release them and notice how they feel when you release them.

Now tighten the muscles in your calves and knees. Hold for a count of 3 and then release them. Notice how you feel.

Now tighten the muscles in your thighs, hamstrings and buttocks.

Hold this area tight for a count of 3. Now release the muscles in this area and notice how you feel.

Now tighten the muscles in your arms, hands and fingers. Make a fist with your hands hold these areas tight for a count of 3.

Now release the muscles in these areas and notice how you feel.

Tighten the muscles in abdomen, stomach, and low back and hold for a count of 3. Now release the muscles in this area.

Now tighten the muscles in your solar plexus, mid back, and chest area and hold for a count of 3. Now release the muscles in these areas and notice how you feel.

Tighten the muscles in your shoulders, upper chest, throat and neck areas and hold for a count of 3. Now release the muscles in these areas and notice how you feel.

Now tighten the muscles in your face and head. Scrunch your face together and furrow your eyebrows and forehead for a count of 3.

Now release the muscles in this area and notice how you feel.

Bring your attention and focus back to your heart –lung area and notice how you feel.

Slow your breath down

If any thoughts come into your mind, focus your inner gaze in the heart-lung area and continue to slow your breath down.

Continue to slow your breath down.

Allow your breath to become steadier and calmer

Now, allow yourself to breathe a little deeper, letting the exhalation be a little longer that the inhalation.

Now, begin to breathe in for the count of three, lightly hold for a count of three, and breathe out for a count of three.

Breathe in for a count of three, lightly hold for a count of three, and breathe out for a count of three.

And one more time breathe in for a count of three, lightly hold for a count of three, and breathe out for a count of three.

Your Breath Is the Key to Relaxation and Meditation Pranyama

Breathing and knowing we are breathing is a basic practice. No one can be truly successful in the art of meditating without going through the door of breathing. To practice conscious breathing is to open the door to stopping and looking deeply in order to enter the domain of concentration and insight. Conscious breathing is the way into any sort of meditative concentration. -Thich Nhat Hanh

Your breath is a very important component to your meditation practice; in fact it is integral. Breath awareness is key to the meditative state. In the words of the third century meditation master of the Dyana School Tang Hoi, "Anapanasati, which means being aware of breathing, is the great vehicle offered by the Buddhas to living beings". I emphasis this here, because without conscious breathing there is no meditation practice or meditative state.

Your **breath** is the key to relaxation and inner connectedness.

There is no true meditation or meditative state without breath awareness.

The breath and focus awareness gets you to this state. The breath deepens this state.

Write this down. Imprint this into your mind, make it indelible.

Yes, your breath *is* the key.

There is no way to be relaxed unless your breath is relaxed, breathing full into the diaphragm, evenly paced and slow.

Ever notice an infant breathing? Full body breaths, deep into the diaphragm, evenly paced and slow, whether sleeping or awake.

If your breath is not relaxed you cannot be physiologically and mentally relaxed. They go hand in hand. I say physiologically relaxed because you elicit the relaxation response; which is a physical response elicited by meditation. This means you begin to positively control the autonomic nervous system (involuntary part of the nervous system where stress response is elicited. -flight or fight.)

We can't control the autonomic nervous system. It is an involuntary response to perceived harm, actual harm or life threatening situations. This is one of the places stress, actually over stress or dis-stress, originates from physiologically.

We can positively influence this process, alleviating or abating the stress through the process of meditation.

When you slow your breath down and begin breathing slowly and rhythmically the muscles along the throat, esophagus, heart-lung area, stomach, abdomen, spinal column begin to relax and release.

What was once constricted or tense begins to release.

We cannot will or force ourselves to relax by self-coercion. We can however work in conjunction with our breath and mind to create relaxation and therefore health and healing. Just the mere action of focusing on your breath begins a process of relaxation.

This simple meditation I have taught to countless of my patient/clients to foster great health and stress reduction.

Many cardiologists have been prescribing breath work for years and now there is more wide spread use of this effective technique that you can carry with you w here ever you go.

Breath work greatly oxygenates your body, massages your internal organs and calms your mind bringing you into a centered state.

There are many cases of lowered blood pressure as well as relief from anxiety from any of the breath work meditations.

Breath work and meditation go hand in hand. There is no way to separate the two. There are integral components to each part of the process of meditation, as well as yoga.

Think of these meditations as money in the bank. The more you put in the more you have. Or, anything that you are learning or studying. The more you do it, the easier it is to do. And in the case of meditation you build a nice platform to tap into. In fact, you can get to a point where this is your 'everyday living state.'

The point to this little book is to show you how to access the meditative state and live more and more consistently in this state of being and awareness.

The focus now is just to begin to familiarize yourself with the process of meditation. Taking life and learning one step at a time and being process orientated create a state of mind that greatly reduces stress.

Enjoy the process, watch it flow and see where it takes you

 C3

The Yogic Breath
(The breath of union body and mind)

This breath creates union through breath awareness and this breath is foundational to all the meditation practices. Unless stated otherwise use this breath in all meditations. This breath is also considered more of a yang breath meaning that it is more active. In eastern traditions the term yang is that which is of the male principle-more active, outwardly and energizing. Yin would be that which is more focused inward, slow and calming.

One simple example would be the sun would be considered yang. The moon yin. The day yang and the night yin.

(Pranayama- In the Hindu spiritual tradition rhythmic breathing is called pranayama. There are many forms. Remember the word form… We will go into 5 basic forms that are the foundation of most meditation practices.)

It is said in the many traditions of meditation that if your breath is steady and calm your mind will be steady and calm.

Your mind follows the state of your breath.

A steady breath a calm mind.

Try this and see:

Right now as you are reading this just begin to focus on your breath and notice how you are breathing. Simply read these words and notice how you are breathing. Just become more aware of your breath without trying to change it. First just notice it as you read.

Now begin to consciously slow your breath down. Let your out breath be a little bit longer than your in breath; almost like an inward and subtle sigh. Perhaps sit a little straighter. Just straighten your body so that you are more upright and notice how you feel. Notice any subtle or obvious changes in your breath or how you are feeling.

Now relax your shoulders, allow your chin to slightly drop in towards your chest. This opens up the back of your neck and stretches your spine. Do this with ease, no force is needed. You need not touch your chin to your chest, just a natural relaxing of your head, neck and shoulders. Make sure your jaw is relaxed and breathe with your mouth in a relaxed position. Breathe through your nose slowly and calmly. Continue to slow your breath down.

Close your eyes and focus your attention on your heart-lung area.

Simply watch your breath.

Noticing each inhalation and each e x halation.

Now, breathe more deeply, begin to breathe into your diaphragm.

Breathe easily into your solar plexus and abdomen.

Now, as you breathe into your solar plexus and abdomen engaging your diaphragm allow your belly to fill with the air of your breath.

You will feel a slight ballooning sensation. Allow this with comfort and ease.

Now, as you breathe out slightly and lightly draw your abdominal muscles toward your spinal column.

Continue this pattern of breathing as you focus your inner gaze into your heart and lung area.

Continue to breathe slowly and evenly paced as you focus inward watching your breath.

ೞ

The 3 Part Breath

Continue the yogic breath with the added awareness of breathing into your face. Feel the muscles in your face flush with your breath.

Now draw your breath into your heart-lung area (the chest)

Now draw your breath into the diaphragm, solar plexus, and abdomen area.

As you breathe out be aware of your breath now going out of your abdomen, solar plexus, and diaphragm.

Now feel the breath going out of your heart-lung area and now out of your facial area.

So you are breathing in and drawing your breath down from your face and throat into your heart-lung area and then into the diaphragm, solar plexus and abdominal area.

As you breathe out you shift your awareness upward while drawing your abdominal muscles slightly in while your awareness focus on your diaphragm, then your heart-lung area and then your facial area.

Do this for a cycle of 5-6 times. You can build up to more.

☙

The 4 Part Breath

This breath is very similar to the 3 Part Breath.

In this breath work you are accessing another part of your body and mind called a transcendent state.

This state encompasses the body; yet goes beyond the denser physical body. The breath greatly activates and connects one to one's subtle energy. All you really need know is that it feels good and brings a lot of clarity of mind. It can be wonderful for pain relief or relief of headaches.

Now begin to consciously slow your breath down. Let your out breath be a little bit longer than your in breath; almost like an inward and subtle sigh. Perhaps sit a little straighter. Just straighten your body so that you are more upright and notice how you feel. Notice any subtle or obvious changes in your breath or how you are feeling.

Now relax your shoulders, allow your chin to slightly drop in towards your chest. This opens up the back of your neck and stretches your spine. Do this with ease, no force is needed. You need not touch your chin to your chest, just a natural relaxing of your head, neck and shoulders. Make sure your jaw is relaxed and breath with your mouth slightly closed. Breath through your nose slowly and calmly. Continue to slow your breath down.

Now, breath more deeply. Begin to breath into your diaphragm.

Breathe easily into your solar plexus and abdomen.

Now, as you breathe into your solar plexus and abdomen engaging your diaphragm allow your belly to fill with the air of your breath.

You will feel a slight ballooning sensation. Allow this with comfort and ease.

Now, as you breathe out slightly and lightly draw your abdominal muscles toward your spinal column.

Now as you continue to slow your breath down bring you focus to the top of your head and notice how you feel.

Become very aware of the top of your head and notice how that part of your body feels. You may feel a tingling sensation, or you may not feel anything in particular. Just notice without judgment and be aware.

Now be aware of your breath coming from the top of your head and visualize your breath coming into your head, your forehead, and throat and into your heart- lung area.

Now draw your breath into your diaphragm, solar plexus, and abdomen area.

As you are breathing in allow your abdomen to fill with your breath and as you breath out gently draw your abdominal muscles toward your spinal column.

As you breath out drawing your abdominal muscles toward your spinal column releasing the breath all the way from the abdominal cavity, up through the heart-lung area, into the throat, face and out through the top of your head

As you breathe in your breath draw the breath down from the top of your head, filling into the facial area, heart-lung area and into the abdominal cavity filling the areas with your breath.

Continue this process slowly and evenly for a cycle of 5-6 times.

Notice how you feel. You may even want to write down your experience. It is up to you. Do what feels right for you to aid in your healing process.

☙

The 3 Count Breath

Allow yourself to get into a comfortable relaxed position.

Sit or lie down in a way that your body feels comfortable.

Close your eyes and bring your inner gaze into the heart-lung area.

Slow your breath down. Allow your breath to slow down.

Breathe slowly and easily all the way into your diaphragm, solar plexus and abdomen.

As you inhale allow your abdominal cavity to fill with your breath.

As you exhale draw your abdominal muscles lightly and easily back toward your spinal column.

Relax the muscles in your head, neck and shoulders as you continue to slow your breath down.

Now, breathe in for a count of 3

Breathe in slowly and easily for a count of 3

Now, hold lightly and easily for a count of 3

Now, release your breath all the way out for a count of 3

Breathe in deeply and easily for a count of 3

Now, hold lightly and easily as you go deeper inside for a count of 3

Now, release your breath slowly and easily for a count of 3

Do this for a cycle of 5 – 6 times

ℭℬ
The Yin Breath

This breath is has a very determined inward focus and is used for calming.

It also has been known to benefit the kidneys and calm and balance emotions.

In oriental medicine the kidneys have a correlation with our emotions.

In Eastern traditions the term yang is that which is of the male principle-more active, outwardly and energizing. Yin would be that which is more focused inward, slow and calming.

Some simple examples would be:

The sun would be considered yang. The moon yin. The day yang and the night yin. Hot would be yang and cool would be yin.

An outward focus would be considered yang and an inward focus yin.

I suggest you do this meditation in a quiet and calm place.

This meditation is helpful when you have a lot of outer demands and concerns and really want to go deeply within.

The focus is completely inward and is to be done with eyes closed. (Eventually, later in your practice you can take this out into your everyday living and do with your eyes open, even in line at a store or bank)

Sit in a comfortable relaxed position either in a crossed - legged position or with your feet on the floor.

Close your eyes and focus on your heart-lung area.

Begin to slow your breath down.

Adjust your body in a way that you feel more comfortable inside.

Begin to breathe deeply from the left to the right side of your body.

Breathe into your solar plexus, abdomen, oblique muscles (sides of your abdomen), the focus and direction of your breath is lateral (from side to side).

You can even visualize yourself breathing from the left to right side of your body. Visualize your breath moving from each side of your body and feel your attention focusing deeper inside. As your attention is focused deeper inside your awareness is drawn deeper inside.

Continue the yin breath - lateral breathing until you feel more calm, centered and a deepening of your inward focus.

Inner Work – Growth Work for Inner State Awareness & Pranyama (breath)

Dyana/Vipassana – Samatha-Samadhi (basic translation-from awareness of what is, being in the present moment leads to oneness, connectedness- no separation-God consciousness-the truth of who you are, One pointedness, one with the eternal, Spiritual Beingness.

This *awareness of what is* or dyana vipassana (Sanskrit/Buddhist) without a projection of judgment, fear or comparison brings one into a harmony of the present moment.

When you couple your awareness of what is with a relaxed yogic breath you begin to arrive at a state of being of total connectedness, eternal nature or samatha -samadhi (Sanskrit/Buddhist)

With dyana and your breath awareness or pranyama, samatha or Samadhi is a natural by product. All you need to do is notice, observe, watch and bring your attention and focus back to your breath.

This one pointed ness, oneness, connectedness, feeling and awareness of no separation comes from connecting in with a non-dualistic state of consciousness.

In Eastern philosophy and teachings it is thought that all pain stems from duality. Wanting to leave something or go to something. Being too hot, or too cold, loving someone or something, hating someone or something. When we are so for something we elicit the opposite of being so against something.

This is our human nature and the play of the little mind. This is not our True Nature. Our True Nature is beyond duality and yet takes the dual nature into account. The little mind, the rational mind likes to rationalize and analyze. Again, this has its place in moderation and balance. Too much analyzing brings worry, too little brings folly. It is said that most of our problems stem from imbalance, from a quality or situation that is taken too far and hence creates stress in one area.

In meditation you learn to allow your True Nature to come through the ego mind. The ego mind then takes the back seat so to speak while infinite mind comes through.

Now that you have been practicing your breath work and are aware of your breath I'd like you to bring this awareness to your everyday living. This meditation process will help you separate out the truth of who you are. You will begin to see you are not your thoughts, your feelings, your house, your car, your job, your worry, you are even not your meditation practice, religion, philosophy or beliefs.

You use these, express through these, but your True Nature includes these and goes beyond.

Students of mine as well as private spiritual life coaching clients of mine have used this meditation process for many uses.

Some while walking, some while in an argument with a mate; others in the workforce. You can even use this while driving or standing in a long line at the store. You can do this with your eyes close or open.

Hopefully, you will get to a point where this process kicks in at times when you need more awareness and you are able to use this to create more peace of mind. This meditation process greatly reduces stress and teaches your mind to follow your breath. You begin to get conscious control of your thoughts through this innerwork.

This meditation process teaches you thoughts come and go. Feelings come and go. The one true constant is your breath.

This can show you the impermanence of things. Are thoughts and feelings are impermanent. They change. All of life is change.

Our True Nature is Changeless. And, therefore the one dependable constant in our life.

Take some time to just sit and watch your thoughts.

With each thought or group of thoughts simply notice your thoughts and then bring your attention and focus back to your breath.

Notice what you are thinking and bring your attention and focus back to your breath.

You can even say in your mind "dyana" and then bring your attention and focus back to your breath.

Continue to just watch, be aware of your thoughts, your feelings without judgment or trying to change how you feel or what you are thinking.

Be aware of sounds around you and then bring your attention and focus back to your breath.

Be aware of your mind, your body, how your body is feeling.

Notice any annoyances.

Just notice and be aware- dyana

Continue your yogic breath. Continue to slow your breath down.

Now just breathe. Just notice what and how you think and feel and then notice your breath. Just notice you are breathing and how you are breathing without judgment or trying to change anything.

Note your insight and experiences in your meditation journal.

Breathing in Peace

Mindfulness and conscious breathing are sources of energy that can calm the storm of anger, which itself is also a source of energy.
-Thich Nhat Hahn

It is so interesting and synchronistic that when I went to write this meditation *I* needed it the most. So many of my client's remark how peaceful I am and how "I walk my talk". Yes, I do; however not without challenges and having to do the same processes and meditations that I suggest to them. Peace is a state that is very often disturbed and worn away by attrition. It can happen in small increments, and before we know it our peaceful state has evaporated.

Peace does not mean "no issues", challenges, problems or obstacles.

Peace means a deep recognition and a connection through feeling to that perfect, calm, still spot within.

There are days and weeks when all is going 'wrong' and I feel completely peaceful with a sense of joy within. There are other days when I strive for my peace. On those days it is either hard won like a tennis match between my ego mind (bless its soul and agenda), or I simply surrender and watch the game stating in my mind "This too shall pass." The up, happy times as well as the sad down times all pass. Nothing stays the same in this world. Change is the only constant. The only state that doesn't change is change and the only part of us that doesn't change is our true essence.

❧

Breathing in Peace Meditation

Allow yourself to just stop what you are doing.

Adjust your body so that it is in a more comfortable, relaxed position.

Close your eyes.

Begin to focus on your breath. Notice how you are breathing.

Now, slow your breath down. Continue to slow your breath down.

And now integrate your yogic breathing.

Breathing deep into your abdominal cavity filling it with the breath of life, your life.

This is your life. And a time for you to take care.

Allow your breath to become steady and calm.

Continue to slow your breath down.

Now begin to picture and imagine that you are breathing in peace.

How would it feel to feel peace now?

Picture and imagine this feeling of peace entering into you like waves of light.

Breathe in peace and breathe out any tension.

With each in breath you are breathing in peace and light.

With each out breath you are releasing tension and stress.

If you can, picture and imagine a blue ray of light washing over you like a cool- warm wave that feels so good inside.

Breathe in peace from the top of your head to the tips of your toes.

Feel this peace present within.

Connecting With the Detached Observer - The Witness Self

"You don't need eyes to see you need vision" -DJ Faithless

It is not until we can detach, back up, so to speak that we can get clarity and clearly see what is going on in our life and around us. So often we are "poised to act", or react. Many times we are reacting to what has happened in the past, what we want to happen or fear will happen. When we can get clarity to "really see" we go beyond the eyes and into a knowingness to really see. In order to clearly see, beyond the eyes (surface appearances) and connect in with this inner knowing we need to detach from overly emotional or intellectual states and connect with the witness self to truly see. This is vision.

This meditation is so crucial to any spiritual development and integration program. It is an integral part of any spiritual practice and is desperately needed in our modern times. So many of our issues are because we become *too* emotionally entangled in situations.

Balance and temperance are key components to peace of mind.

We can, no matter what is going on around us and challenging our preferred state of mind, create a mental state that allows us to disengage and attain clarity. Yes, it is possible on a regular basis.

Again, this does take practice. And that is what meditation is- a mental practice to do over and over. Practice makes perfect. Well, as perfect as can be in this perfect/imperfect world.

❧

Connecting With the Detached
Observer Meditation

Allow yourself to sit or lie down in a comfortable relaxed position.

Close your eyes.

Focus your inner vision on the heart-lung area of your body and just notice your breath.

Notice how you are breathing.

Notice how you are feeling.

Slow your breath down

If any thoughts come into your mind, focus your inner gaze in the heart-lung area and continue to slow your breath down.

Continue to slow your breath down.

Allow your breath to become more steady and more calm.

Now, allow yourself to breathe a little deeper, letting the exhalation be a little longer that the inhalation.

As you continue to slow your breath down relax the muscles in your head, neck and shoulders.

Now, begin to breathe in for the count of three, lightly hold for a count of three, and breathe out for a count of three.

Breathe in for a count of three, lightly hold for a count of three, and breathe out for a count of three.

And one more time breathe in for a count of three, lightly hold for a count of three, and breathe out for a count of three.

As you are now feeling more relaxed, allow your breath to go into its own natural rhythmic pattern. Notice how you are breathing.

Bring your attention into your heart-lung area and focus on the space and place in between your inhalation and exhalation. There is a space in between the in breath and the out breath. Focus on that place inside. Now, go a little deeper inside and focus within.

Now, bring your attention and focus to the top of your head. Notice how you feel. Continue to focus on your breath as you also focus on the energy at the top of your head.

Ask yourself: "Who is watching your breath?"

Notice there is a part of you that is observing your breath.

There is a part of you that is always, calm, peaceful, watching and observing. This is your observer self. The witness within.

This part of you is always in a neutral state.

Do this for a while in your own time and mind until you can sense, see, or feel this very important part of you.

The 4 Afflictions of the Mind - The 3 Afflictions of Attitude

It is impossible for a man to conceal himself.

In every act, word, or gesture he stands revealed as he is, and not as he would have himself appear to be. From the universe nothing is or can be hidden. -Ernest Holmes

An *affliction* is something that causes pain or suffering. The word comes from Middle English and originally meant infliction of pain and/or humiliation. When we are caught in the web of our affliction/s we are self -inflicting pain and we can also be humiliating ourselves.

Others may not see this or know this about us. It is our "inner state".

However as Ernest Holmes so profoundly speaks in the words above "From the universe nothing is or can be hidden."

The 4 afflictions of the mind are:

1. Aversion
2. Attachment
3. Suffering over ones "suffering"
4. 4 – Illusion/s

The 3 Afflictions of Attitude are:

1. Fear
2. Comparison
3. Judgment.

The *afflictions of the mind* come from our memory. They are what we are identified with. It is an element of us as a person, since they reside in the surface mind. The afflictions of the mind are our device/s for seeing. In many ways they are how we view life. It is the lens or filter we perceive through. It is the way we see the world and ourselves in it. Are we overly focused on what *we* (ego mind) like or dislike, hence being overly opinionated and confrontational? Are we overly attached to our beliefs, people and or situations? Are we attached to "things staying the same for security"? Are we clinging to a situation or our perception of life? Are we overly suffering over our losses, disappointments and twists of fate? Do we feel a victim to fate? These mindsets reflect the afflictions of the mind.

Afflictions of attitude are from our behavior and way of "thinking". The afflictions of attitude reflect how we think and feel toward ourselves, others and life. It is the attitude we have about life. The afflictions of attitude show are we braced in life or flowing. These afflictions show the posture we take in life. They also show our inner dialogue. Are we stuck or frozen with fear? Do we jump to worse case scenarios? Do we not trust our divine plan and the way our life is unfolding? Are we comparing our life path with other's path? Are we comparing our past with our present? Are we judging our path? Are we overly judging our talents, skills or innate gifts as less than? Are we constantly looking sideways at our friends, colleagues or family thinking, "Why don't *I* have that?" "Why is my life like this, and their life like that?" These attitudes reveal the inner thought process of afflictions of attitude.

Meditation brings to our conscious awareness these afflictions. In the meditative state we can use this awareness to make the changes in our mental state and attitude.

The first step in making positive change is awareness. We can't change or alter what we are not aware of. Many times these afflictions are not in our conscious awareness. They remain subconscious or unconscious to us, even though they impact our life and living. We can change what we become aware of, and even if the predilection remains we can change how we respond to our expression or acting out of these afflictions. Through meditation we go beyond the surface behaviors and thought processes to the state of all knowing and all understanding. In this state we truly arrive at a place of self-love and self-acceptance. The "I Ching", also known, as the "Book of Changes" or book of wisdom, is a book for aligning to the "Wu Wei" or flow of life, calls this a "State of Possession in Great Measure". The "I Ching", which is a bit of an Eastern, based (Chinese Philosophy) road map for life stresses self-development, spiritual integration and the use of meditation. This road map is a constant in any solid spiritual practice. We need self-development and spiritual integration and a balance of study with meditation to tap into our inner knowing and true nature. In this state of "Possession in Great Measure". We realize that all that we need is right inside us. We are whole perfect in spirit and form.

"Possession in Great Measure is an inner independence from having overcome self –pity. "Possession in Great Measure" is an inner knowing and inner connectedness to our Spirit, God, All That Is and the Flow of All Life. "Possession of Great Measure" is a knowingness and connectedness to the truth that what we have within cannot be taken from us, cannot be lost in spite of temporary setbacks in life. It is the realization of our true nature, our spiritual nature, the part of us that is immortal, and a part of the All That Is of the Universe.

The afflictions of mind and attitude block the inner truth of our "Possession in Great Measure". The good news is that this blockage is part of the illusion...For the truth is whether we are aware of our True Nature or not it is still present and within us and expressing as us. This is our spiritual nature and this nature is innate. It is there whether we know it or not. We are spiritual beings living out through form. Life is just a lot more calm, stress free, interesting, magical, mystical, and fulfilling with conscious awareness of our True Nature.

The afflictions are listed here to help you become even more self aware through your meditation practice. My hope is that through your meditation practice you will be able to connect into to your true nature and that the afflictions will be seen for what they are- fleeting and transitory states of mind and attitude.

1) *Aversion*- Being so against something. It is a strong dislike, hatred of, distaste, abhorrence, or hostility. When we are stuck in an "aversion to something or someone" we are not in the present moment and we are poised "against". An aversion sets up a polarity in our mind and in our life experience. When we are so for or against something or someone we create an experience of separation. We are no longer in an awareness of "oneness". We also are not in an aligned and centered state, as we are polarized. In the Buddhist philosophy it is said to be in the "Middle Way"—neither for nor against, happy or sad. It is in this state that we find peace. In the bible it is said, "This

too shall pass." Passions and emotions come and go. They are fleeting as the temporal world. Our true state, our inner nature is neutral and centered in peace. We can experience and express through our emotions. We can have like and dislikes or preferences. This is our human nature, this is the realm of the ego-mind, the personality self. This is an important and many times fun part of life; however we don't' want to be overly tied to our passions, likes and dislikes.

Remember the saying "Never say never." When we are stuck in an aversion/s we steel ourselves away from the possibility of authentic self expression, because we have put out there to others and the universe "I never would, could, etc." We don't know what we could or would do. We don't always know what wants to be expressed through us. When we change it is an inside job that we can either facilitate through awareness or try and stop through holding on to an old point of view or paradigm.

The remedy for the affliction of aversion is dispassion. To calm the mind, connect in be centered inside. This is done through meditation. Many think that to be centered or follow the "Middle Way" is to be cut off from one's emotions or not have passion. This is so far from the truth. I am Latin, and I have a lot of passion!!! However in my core I feel peaceful. I feel a state and experience of connectedness and a quiet calm. Whether angry, happy, sad, uncertain or feeling on top of the world I know this "too shall pass", and this is ok. This is the play of consciousness of the material world. I know my eternal nature is unchanging and all that is of spirit is stable and dependable.

So, I "like" when situations are easy and there is a good flow for me in my life, but I have learned, and continue to learn this experience to not have a strong hatred or dislike for the opposite experience.

Attachment- The condition of being *overly* attached. Linked up, being fixed or fastened to something or someone.

It is natural and normal to bond, to have a fondness for something or someone. This is a wonderful part of our life on earth. It is human nature to get cozy and comfy with our ideas and beliefs. Many times we feel if something worked in the past it has got to work now and into the future. The issue is we change…life changes, our focus, our priorities change and most importantly the spirit within us from a soul level likes to expand its mode of expression. If we allow it there is a divine flow of spiritual energy that is emerging through us for the most fulfillment in our life. If we are overly attached to the past, present, or a certain situation remaining a certain way we cut off the divine flow. We can even be attached to a focus on the future.

So, we want to connect, to feel and express love through bonding. There is a balance between being attached and yet open to the unfolding of life and one's life path. Not always easy, and yet really it is true reality. The one constant in life is change. With meditation one can mediate this change. One can be aware of the change that is emerging through one's being and life. Through meditation we can heal the wounds that keep us stuck in the past. It is in aligning to our true nature that we move beyond the change to the changeless.

The truth is that we are always connected to each other in spirit. This connecting never ends and lives on. This connecting is our life force. It is the life force, prana of all of life forms and expression.

The remedy for *Attachment is Detachment*. I like to call this remedy "Detached Compassion". We are connected. We love; and if we lose someone through crossing over (death) or moving on from our life, we are sad, we grieve. We feel the loss of the physical presence. We allow this sadness and grieving and yet we are able to still feel the connection and we have the awareness of the truth of our ultimate connection. There is a knowingness and feeling of this connection.

Illusion - We can get caught up in illusions. An illusion is a false idea or belief. It is a manifestation of the rational or surface mind. The surface mind sees surface reality and believes it to be so. The surface mind tells us it was this way in the past it will be this way in the future. The surface mind only knows what we input.

Garbage in = Garbage out.

The surface mind houses about as much information as a hard drive.... and old school hard drive at that!! It houses about 7.8 bits of information.

The rational, logical, analytical mind is great. A great tool; It is like a sailboat.... You need the "Higher Mind" "Divine Mind", "Creative Mind" "The Mind of Expanded Consciousness" to sail the boat.

In meditation we connect into this expanded consciousness. This is the rudder we want to steer the boat.

The remedy for *illusion is Spiritual Discernment.* Through meditation and living in a meditative state more and more we see more clearly.

We really begin to see the true nature of reality. We begin to see beyond the surface reality of life. We begin to know and trust our spiritual nature and inner knowing. In the experience of material reality there are problems and issues. In the expression of spirit there is only perfection. It is not so much what happens to us, but how we respond to it.

A client of mine once said "I have this pattern I have been trying and trying to change. Now, I see it is not so much me changing my pattern, but how I respond to it."

This is true wisdom. We all have a blueprint, a plan and a purpose we come into this life with. We all are unique and individual and have a distinct way of living and being.

Our inherent pattern is unchangeable. We can change and alter some ways of relating and being; however some is our innate way of expressing this lifetime, if you will.

If we can move beyond the illusion of separation and imperfection we will see and experience our life as perfect and integral to the balance of all life.

In the words of the contemporary mystic and meditation teacher Osho:

"Witnessing will not change your conditioning. Witnessing will not change your body musculature. But witnessing will give you an experience that you are beyond all musculature, all conditioning. In that moment of beyondness, in that moment of transcendence, no problem exists."

Through the practice of meditation and living more and more in the meditative state you realize you are not just your body, you are not just your mind. You experience and express through your body and mind. This is the place beyond illusion and delusion. This is the place of discernment to see and experience the Truth of Who You Are....

Suffering over Ones Suffering- We've all been here. I know I have.

We are going through an awful situation, spiritually and metaphysically it is called a "Dark night of the soul", and we wallow in it….. Some call this "victim consciousness" Now, I am a therapist and I do acknowledge we need to, and it is healthy to process or cycle through our "painful situations". There are no kudos at the end of the day or life for "keeping a stiff upper lip" and plowing through a situation, steeling us from the pain or suffering. However, there can be a tendency; especially in the Western world to become so focused on what we "Don't have", "Our needs and wants", and our personal "troubles" that we lose sight of the blessings.

The remedy for *Suffering over one's suffering is Generating Goodwill.*

Generating goodwill allows us to take the focus off of our "problem" and us. I once called a good friend of mine to lament my woes with him, and commiserate a bit… Yes, I can still do this "human thing" ☺

I usually, make a habit of checking in with the person to see if it is a good time to talk, and to see what frame of mind before going into "my stuff". I asked my friend how he was doing and he started explaining to me his concern and worry over his little animal being (doggy) that was in the hospital and might have a serious disease.

He then asked me "Why? What's up?" I said "Never mind. I called to complain and your problem with your little animal being makes mine seem very minor now!" When he told me his situation all I could think about was: "Michele, you are so lucky Yoshi (my doggy-animal being) is so healthy." I kept seeing her bright sunny little face and felt such appreciation. I let go and was present for my friend and his situation and we ended up having an amazing conversation and laughed and laughed throughout our conversation. It seems I ended up being the recipient of my goodwill cycling back to me.

Goodwill can also be expressed through heartfelt gratitude. A walking meditation of being aware of your blessings really helps cure this.

I like to write a gratitude list and/or send an email of appreciation to friends, family and clients. I have even sent anonymous gifts of money or other goodies to friends that were in need when my coffers felt extra full. Another wonderful meditation is to contemplate all that you feel grateful for and appreciative of in your life. As you are focusing on the people, the situations, the loves of your life breath in the feeling of the gratitude and as you breathe out allow this feeling of gratitude to be felt in the whole of your body and being through your breath.

The 3 afflictions of attitude manifest as fear, comparison or judgment.

When we are in a fear state, thinking fear thoughts and feeling fearful we paralyze ourselves. There is a fear that is useful. The body can give us a message of fear that lets us know danger is ahead or that a stove is too hot to touch. This is healthy fear; however living in a state of fear is unhealthy as it blocks, stops, and holds back our spiritual energy and expression.

The affliction of comparison has us looking at everyone's path, but our own. In this attitude we are overly focused on "the other". We appreciate or want what others have without an appreciation for our unique path. Comparison is like a ping-pong game- we are constantly looking from side to side. This type of attitude and living drains our life force. We can become depressed by what we think we don't have, and perhaps think we should have.

The attitude affliction of judgment stunts our self-expression and causes us to overly self-focus. Unfortunately it isn't a self-focus of love, appreciation or acknowledgment, but one of recrimination. For many this attitude of judgment becomes a protection mechanism. One is afraid to slip up or make a mistake.

One is overly cautious, overly analyzing and overly aware. This also dwindles the life force energy. There begins to be an implosion of energy. This can lead to depression and a feeling of what is the use because of the judgment that one is not measuring up. And, I would ask "Measuring up to what and whom?" There is no one to measure up to, as we are needed on this planet as is... Our individual expression is an important part to the whole, the whole of life. Meditation opens us up to this and lets us not only see this, but feel this and life this. This is the state of connectedness we all seek to live in. This state allows a life of centeredness, contentment and inner peace.

Driving and Breath Awareness

Meditation can be practiced almost anywhere- While sitting, walking, lying down, standing, even while working, drinking and eating. There are many forms of meditation. -Thich Nhat Hahn

Yes, you can be meditate and align to meditative state while driving.

Meditation is awareness and the more relaxed you are the more aware you are.

Most of the time we experience extra stress while driving because we are overly focused on one aspect of the drive. Usually it is traffic or "time"

The focus of the mind is on running late- Am I running late?

"Do I have enough time?" Time is like a watching a pot boil.

A watched pot takes longer to boil, or at least *seems* like it does. And, so is the case with driving the more you watch and focus on the limiting factors the drive seems longer and is definitely more stressful.

Meditation is a form of awareness that elicits the relaxation response and brings one in tune whether their inner state of being. The part of you that is beyond the rush hour traffic or the frustration of a backed up freeway lane.

The purpose of this mediation is to bring your relaxed awareness in all aspects of your life. Driving and being in traffic just one place you can use to practice breath awareness and relaxation.

Remember the more relaxed you are the more aware.

☙

Driving and Breath Awareness Meditation

While sitting in your car adjust your body position so that your lumbar region (low back) is flush to the back of the car seat. If your car won't accommodate this body position a very small pillow, or rolled up sock between the small of your back and the car seat can aid in this.

Put both feet flat on the floor in front of you and adjust your body so that you are in a relaxed upright position. Make sure that your hips are squared and evenly positioned forward. You don't want one hip slightly more forward than the other.

Make sure that you are seated in a way that your arms are not overextended while on the steering wheel. You may have to adjust your seat.

Now, relax into the back of the seat.

Allow your shoulders to relax downward and make sure that your head is not jutting forward with your chin over protruding out from your head.

This causes undue stress on your neck.

Now, begin to breathe deeply and slowly breathing fully into your abdominal cavity.

You are now ready to drive.

While you are drive continue to notice how you are breathing and keep your breath slow and evenly paced.

Notice if while in traffic there are any changes in your breath.

You can consciously slow your breath down, breath slower and more deeply if you experience any stress.

Just notice, be aware and consciously slow your breath down.

This will automatically counter any dis-stress.

Ascension Meditation- Accessing Your Inner Guidance

The second aspect of God is Chit (Sanskrit), which means cosmic intelligence or knowledge. Chit is also called Chiti, which is Universal Consciousness. Chiti is that which at all times and in all places manifests or discloses everything as it is. -Swami Muktananda

In this meditation you are rising above duality to the place of inner calm & union. This is the place and space of "inner knowing" We can't receive inner guidance or access our inner knowing when we are not balanced or are overly stressed poised for action. In this rising above duality we are expanding our consciousness to go beyond the place in the mind of limiting and self-serving thoughts and considerations.

Ascending or rising above is not floating in the sky or escaping it is bringing in the opposite thought, idea or experience and moving into the middle plan. It is moving beyond extremes. It is a space beyond small mindedness, ego likes and dislikes. It is a place beyond "I'm right and you are wrong."

In the words of the mystic poet Rumi "Out there beyond the ideas of right and wrong doing there is a field… I'll meet you there."

Our inner knowing is here. It is beyond our likes and dislikes, our pettiness. It includes this, but doesn't remain stuck in the limitation.

Our Inner guidance goes to the truth, the heart of the matter; which is always a little bit of both, right there in the center, in the middle way. This is the "Tao"; the flow of life is neither to close to the left or too far to the right.

It is just right. Right in the middle. The middle way.

This inner guidance may call us into non-action; and yet in "not acting" we are acting. There is right action in non-action. This does not mean procrastination or putting off. It means using the higher mind to receive the input of when to physically act.

We are always in some form of action, if just mentally or on the inner plane. To consciously not act is an action.

Action for Action sake is not empowered action, but reaction.

❧

Ascension Meditation

Allow yourself to sit or lie down in a comfortable relaxed position.

Close your eyes.

Focus your inner vision on the heart-lung area of your body and just notice your breath.

Notice how you are breathing.

Notice how you are feeling.

Slow your breath down

If any thoughts come into your mind, focus your inner gaze in the heart-lung area and continue to slow your breath down.

Continue to slow your breath down.

Allow your breath to become more steady and more calm

Now, allow yourself to breathe a little deeper, letting the exhalation be a little longer that the inhalation.

As you continue to slow your breath down relax the muscles in your head, neck and shoulders.

Now, begin to breathe in for the count of three, lightly hold for a count of three, and breathe out for a count of three.

Breathe in for a count of three, lightly hold for a count of three, and breathe out for a count of three.

And one more time breathe in for a count of three, lightly hold for a count of three, and breathe out for a count of three.

As you are now feeling more relaxed, allow your breath to go into its own natural rhythmic pattern. Notice how you are breathing.

Bring your attention into your heart-lung area and focus on the space and place in between your inhalation and exhalation. There is a space in between the in breath and the out breath.

Focus on that place inside.

Now, go a little deeper inside and focus within.

Now, bring your attention and focus to the top of your head.

Notice how you feel.

Continue to focus on your breath as you also focus on the energy at the top of your head.

As you continue to slow your breath down notice how your body is feeling.

As you exhale bring your attention and focus to the very top of your head and picture, imagine or sense and feel a funnel of light going upward from the top of your head.

You might feel a tingly sensation or warmth.

Now, reinforce this funnel of light with your mind's eye and draw your focus and attention 2-3 inches up the funnel of light.

And now move your attention and focus 1 ft. up the funnel of light.

Now, 3 ft, 6ft, 12 ft, 30 ft.

Keep expanding your attention and focus upward 60 ft., 100 ft, 1000 ft. and even more.

Expand your attention and focus 2000ft. However, this feels for you.

Just picture it, image it, feel it, or sense it inside.

Now picture, imagine, sense, see, or feel a source of light.

Now expand your attention and focus into this source of light.

Go as far into this source of light as you want to or can.

Now, feel your connection to this source of light.

And, remember that you are always connected inside.

Feel this connection to the light.

Now, reinforce this connection and bring this light all the way back down inside.

Float and drift down this funnel of light back into your physical body bringing this connection deep inside.

Again, reinforce the funnel of light.

Picture it, imagine it, sense it, see it inside.

This is your connection to your higher awareness, your higher self inside.

Alignment Meditation

Listen carefully; whenever you try to perform something, you are seeking food for the ego. Whenever you are natural and let things happen they are perfect and there is no problem. -Osho

The alignment meditation is a focused meditation. It teaches your mind to focus. This focusing allows you to live in a state of flow. It also after a period of time opens you up to more synchronistic living consciously.

This meditation I do every day. I suggest it to start your day relaxed and balanced. My day is always much more magical when I do this meditation. Everything just flows and I am in right timing. Even if my schedule is off it all ends up being perfect. This is one I would definitely suggest perfecting and practicing on a regular basis. I have also recommended it to so many of my clients with amazing results. Many of my acting clients use this before going on the set. I have one client who religiously uses this alignment meditation before going on stage or even interviews. He has told me he is more relaxed and clearer in thought and noticed a big difference when he doesn't use this tool. He has been using it consistently for about 5 years and swears that it is like a lucky charm for him.

You can also use it to wind down from your day. This meditation is also considered an alignment meditation and aligns you to your higher awareness. It is great even during business meetings or any situation where you need to get more clarity and an objective perspective.

ఁ

Alignment Meditation- Focused Meditation

Take 10-15 minutes for yourself.

Allow yourself to sit or lie down in a comfortable relaxed position.

Close your eyes.

Focus your inner vision on the heart-lung area of your body and just notice your breath.

Notice how you are breathing.

Notice how you are feeling.

Allow yourself to breathe a little deeper, letting the exhalation be a little longer than the inhalation.

Make sure as you are breathing now more slowly that you are relaxing the muscles in your head, neck and shoulders.

Breathe slowing in a relaxed manner, without tensing your muscles or *trying* to force yourself to breathe deeper.

Now, begin to breathe in for the count of three, lightly hold for a count of three, and breathe out for a count of three.

And one more time breathe in for a count of three, lightly hold for a count of three, and breathe out for a count of three.

As you are now feeling more relaxed, allow your breath to go into its own natural rhythmic pattern.

Allow each inhalation to bring in peace, calm and relaxation, and allow each exhalation to release tension and stress.

Notice how you are calm, center and focused inside

From this state, bring your awareness to the top of your head and just notice how you feel.

Expand your attention and awareness 1 ft. above your body.

Now, expand your attention and awareness 3 ft. above your body

From this detached, calm and centered state you can begin your day, or relax your mind to end your day with peace and clarity.

Open Eye Meditation

Seeing things as they are requires a leap, and one can only take this so called leap without leaping from anywhere. If you see from somewhere, you will be conscious of the distance and conscious of the seer as well. -Chogyam Trungpa

This is a wonderful meditation to do in nature, while looking at a tree, a flower or even the ocean. You can also do this indoors with an object. This meditation brings you into present time as well as giving one as sense of connectedness. You can do this meditation while walking, sitting, or lying down.

This meditation trains our mind to align and go into a receptive state even with our eyes open.

Closing our eyes becomes a trigger to relax and we are changing focus and going within. An open eye meditation teaches one to be able to do this at will and to live more and more in this state of being.

I have used this meditation with a candle observing the flame. Earlier on in my practice and training I had a meditation teacher that use to take us to Self Realization Fellowship gardens and we had to pick a tree.

We had to sit in the open eye meditation practice until we connected in awareness to the level that there was no separation between the tree and us. This was an amazing practice.

After many times of this I began to see and feel the connectedness of all of life, every living being and organism. I could feel the oneness. This oneness would be carried with me throughout my day and life experience.

It is a good reminder that we are all life, part of life. We are the comprised of prana life force energy. You can build up to receptivity through this meditation to really see and feel this interconnectedness of all beings and life forms.

❧

Open Eye Meditation Process

While your eyes are open feel your breath.

Notice how you are breathing.

Consciously slow your breath down.

Breathe deeply into your abdominal cavity.

As you breathe in allow your abdominal cavity to fill with your breath.

As you breathe out slightly and lightly draw your abdominal muscles back toward your spinal column.

Continue this rhythm and focus of your breath as you are noticing what is around you.

Continue to slow your breath down.

Notice what you see.

Now focus on one object.

With each inhalation and each exhalation feel and see yourself closer to this object.

See and feel yourself connecting with this object, merging with this object.

Connection with this object or expression of life force.

The Awareness of Now Meditation

Why do you want fruit that is not ripe yet?
-The I Ching-Book of Changes

The fruit of the past is spoiled…. over ripe. It is done. The fruit of the future not yet ripe.

All meditative practices, practice of contemplation or prayer brings us to this understanding and awareness. We can visit the past; envision the future, however we can only live in the present.

In one of my meditations I had the realization- "Where are you going? You have already been in the past and the future isn't here yet.

Yes, where are we all going? And, why are we focused on where we have been. It is gone. It is gone

The "Awareness of Now is quick meditation to bring one into present time.

I have shared this meditation with great success with many of my clients that are going through transition and change. In the process of transition there is the 'gray zone'. The time where we are no longer as connected with the past and our future is not as formed and stable.

This greatly helps to bring ease, peace, and calm in bridging this gap.

Very often we create and generate stress by being overly focused on the past or the future. There is an absence of peace in lamenting over your past or with a preoccupation with your future.

There is so much peace in the present moment. Being in the present moment fully focused on what we are doing aligns us to and creates "the flow state" This flow state creates a calm within and elicits the "relaxation response" releases wonderful endorphins and puts an inward smile on our face.

In the flow state we are not lamenting the past or waging on our future. We are not trying to control outcomes, but in a flow of harmony of being.

And, in truth all that we can control is what is in the moment for us now. We need to all remember that in many ways we create our future moments by our perception and actions in the present. Our future is in many ways built from tiny steps in the present.

What is here is what is right here, right now. Our future will form from our present.

In the legendary words of Ram Dass- "Be here now".

❧

The Awareness of Now Meditation

Notice where you are right now.

Notice what you are doing right now.

Notice what you are focused on right now.

Where are you?

What are you doing?

What are you focused on?

Focus on the now.

Focus all your attention on what you are doing right now.

Focus all your attention on what you are focused on now.

If there is a thought that wants to pull your mind away from what you are doing bring your attention and focus back to the breath.

Now look at what you are doing.

Say in your mind Focus.

❧

Inner Circle Of Light Meditation

Allow yourself to sit or lie down in a comfortable relaxed position.

Close your eyes.

Focus your inner vision on the heart-lung area of your body and just notice your breath.

Notice how you are breathing.

Notice how you are feeling.

Allow yourself to breathe a little deeper, letting the exhalation be a little longer that the inhalation.

Make sure as you are breathing now more slowly that you are relaxing the muscles in your head, neck and shoulders.

Breathe slowing in a relaxed manner, without tensing your muscles or *trying* to force yourself to breathe deeper.

Now, begin to breathe in for the count of three, lightly hold for a count of three, and breathe out for a count of three.

Breathe in for the count of three, lightly hold for a count of three, and breathe out for a count of three.

Breathe in for a count of three, lightly hold for a count of three and breathe out for a count of three.

And one more time breathe in for a count of three, lightly hold for a count of three, and breathe out for a count of three.

Do this until you feel more relaxed inside.

Allow yourself to sit or lie down in a comfortable relaxed position.

Close your eyes.

Focus your inner vision on the heart-lung area of your body and just notice your breath.

Notice how you are breathing.

Notice how you are feeling.

Allow yourself to breathe a little deeper, letting the exhalation be a little longer that the inhalation.

Make sure as you are breathing now more slowly that you are relaxing the muscles in your head, neck and shoulders.

Breathe slowing in a relaxed manner, without tensing your muscles or *trying* to force yourself to breathe deeper.

Now, begin to breathe in for the count of three, lightly hold for a count of three, and breathe out for a count of three.

Breathe in for the count of three lightly hold for a count of three, and breathe out for a count of three.

Continue to breathe in for a count of three, lightly hold for a count of three, and breathe out for a count of three.

Allow each inhalation to bring in peace, calm and relaxation, and allow each exhalation to release tension and stress.

When you are feeling more relaxed, allow your breath to go into its own natural rhythmic pattern.

Now, picture, imagine, sense or feel yourself in a bubble of light.

Sense, see, feel or picture and imagine yourself in a bubble of light calm, centered and focused inside.

Picture and imagine yourself in this bubble of light. Feel this light around you. This bubble of light is a force field of light, a protection of light that acts as a shield of protection.

This bubble of light keeps all the stress outside. You are in your bubble of light, calm and centered inside.

No matter what stress is on the outside you are calm and centered inside.

Now, picture and imagine that your bubble of light is reinforced on the inside allowing you to be more calm and centered inside.

Un-Plug to Plug In

It is said" Don't always let your mind think what it wants to think or your body do what it wants to do."

The idea in this thought is not to cut off from your emotions, feelings or needs of your body. The message in this saying is that you can create conscious control through awareness.

As you grow in your path of self-development and spiritual unfoldment your consciousness evolves to create positive control in your life. Sometimes your mind is going to wander, and you need or want to focus. Sometimes your body is going to be fidgety.

It's like being on an airplane and you "feel" like running up and down the cabin because the flight has been too long. Perhaps you stretch your legs...I don't think you would run up and down the aisle because your body wanted to.

Now, you could bring this feeling into your meditation practice by acknowledging the "feeling" of wanting to run and then consciously bringing your attention back to your breath. You could also create a "mental vacation" and visualize yourself running, and the feeling of the freedom of running and feel that in your body and feel more refreshed and relaxed. How much more empowering is this?

You are now bringing conscious choice into this little situation.

Imagine applying this to all areas of your life?

What would this feel like to you, to have this empowerment of conscious choice?

The feeling of being "disempowered" by external situations or life's demands will be a constant if you can't connect into your higher state of mind, higher consciousness and inner knowing.

If a person is feeling pushed around and controlled by outer situations, the ebb and flow of the needs of others or their own mental –emotional state it will be very difficult to cultivate peace and harmony in their life.

Many times clients and students of mine will exclaim:

"It is so stressful having this cell phone." "My girlfriend calls me all the time when I am meditating." "My family won't let me meditate. "I get so many emails while I am on my computer I can't do my work" "I just see my computer and I have to work." "My husband watches so much TV." "My kids won't talk to me they are constantly gaming and with those video games."

"I can't watch the shopping networks or else I have to buy something."

"My boyfriend keeps texting me."

"This blackberry is running my life." "I'm addicted to my 'crackberry'; I can't put it down."

I also hear "I just can't unplug."

Do you hear the disempowerment and victim stance in all this? I am sure we all could put our own statements together. We each have our own issue in the area of "unplugging." It is wherever there is an imbalance in our lives—too much of a good thing, perhaps.

This can definitely happen in the world of technology.

But, who is running whom? Who is in charge? Who is the conscious being with conscious choice?

Your blackberry doesn't jump into your hands upon arising in the morning. The video game, computer game or Xbox is not glued to your hands. And, your phones do have a mute button and a voice mail.

You can get a handle on this and still enjoy technology. One of my nicknames is "techy mystic" I love high tech-gadgets, computers and recording equipment. I record my own audio meditation CDs, a radio program, podcasting and I do a bit of sound editing.

I love my blackberry—great invention. I love my computers.

I can even appreciate a well tuned engine or the lines of a beautifully designed house, piece of furniture or car.

I also, really love what is behind all the great low and high tech—A creative mind. All of these inventions came from a mind that was in a flow and creating.

You can't be in a creative flow and be "plugged" into external demands constantly. Flow is an inner state that you attune to. You can't be overly attached to the external to align to your inner flow. You have to "unplug" to "plug in"

In this world of constant stimuli it is important to make a conscious effort and create an environment where you can "unplug" every now and then. MTV, the cable music station even has program called "Unplugged". There is a reason for this. Sometimes we need to take the sound down. We don't always need our life amplified.

Many people are addicted to the amplification in their life. They are addicted to the constant stimuli. Technology is not the "problem" The problem is a fear of meeting oneself and being oneself. If you really "meet yourself" and deal with what is there with self love and self acceptance then you may have to actually be your self- your true self.

Many try and use technology to solve the inner problem or issue, whatever this may be for the individual. Just like with any addiction, experience of co-dependence there is an inner need not being met by their person and they are going to external situation and people to meet this need.

Some people also fear slowing down for a bit- What will they encounter?

Their own thoughts… Their own feelings… Themselves.

So, I suggest you to unplug every once in a while. You can explain this to your family, your friends, boyfriend, girlfriend, kids husband, wife. In fact, once this is explained to children they will take their own "quiet time" or "down time." Communication is key for you to be able to unplug.

You set an intention at the beginning of this book. So, I invite you to make another intention. The intention to consciously unplug to plug into you, your inner you.

You can also focus your attention on this intention by turning the ringer off when you need to refresh or renew.

You could also, set some boundaries around your phone, treo pda or blackberry or another device of this sort.

You don't have to have your phone on *all* the time.

It is ok to let a call go to voicemail.

The following is a fun little meditation process that really brings awareness to the feelings and your inner state around the issue of your tech gadgets, land line phones, answer machines, beepers and cell phones.

❧
Unplugging to Plug In Meditation

You can either do this on your own or have help from willing friends or family. Most family members will love to help on this; especially children.

Designate some time for yourself and set an intention to allow time for you to "unplug" to "plug' in- tune into your inner you. Do this in a space where you would normally have some distractions come up.

Do the "Breathing in peace" or one of the other short meditations and/or breath awareness in this book.

Have your cell phone in view, your blackberry and also be near your computer. Whatever the "charged" tech items are for you have them I plane view. You can even have your cell phone in your pocket.

Now, as you are slowing your breath down and focusing in the heart lung area look around at this objects. Really look at them, take them in and bring your attention and focus back to your breath.

You can look at these objects and keep your eyes open and bring your awareness to your breath, or you can close your eyes after viewing the items, and focus on your breath.

Continue this focusing meditation and breath awareness until you get more and more comfortable with the items around you. Do this until you know longer feel the impulse or compulsion "to do" something or "not do something" because these items are on and around you.

The next level of this meditation process is to continue the process and have someone call you, text you, beep you or email you. Or, all of the afore mentioned.

Do this until you feel relaxed and detached from having "missed' the call, or that the phone rang or someone beeped you.

Take time on this and be patient. You may be undoing years of programming, but remember you can un-program by bringing consciousness awareness to your responses.

The first step in change is becoming aware. Once you are aware of your inner triggering you can breathe through it. Bring the breath to the feelings of having to do something. This lessens the compulsion to act or brace oneself to not act.

With this meditation process you will be begin to see and feel that you do have conscious choice.

You can say "no" to the external demands, and yes to your inner connecting.

You can unplug and plug in at will and with time and consistency this will become effortless and second nature.

Partner Meditation

But Let there be spaces in your togetherness, and let the winds
of the heavens dance between you.
And stand together, yet not too near together:

For the pillars of the temple stand apart, and the oak tree and the
cypress tree grow not in each other's shadow. -Kahlil Gibran

This is a wonderful meditation for all kinds of relationships.

It helps the two parties to come into alignment and have a unified intention. It can be used to enhance intimacy.

I have seen it successfully used in business relationships to get the partners in sync and clear the air without having to have lengthy discussions.

Another wonderful use for this meditation is in personal relationships. It brings two people closer together and can heal communication issues.

This meditation can be done between two people or even a group. So, whether friends, business associates or intimate life partners this meditation is a wonderful bridge inner and outer bridge.

❧

Partner Meditation Process

With your partner sit in front of each other about 3 feet apart.

You can sit on the floor in a crossed legged position or in chairs with your feet on the floor. If your feet can't comfortably touch the floor put a pillow on the floor so that your feet are on a flat surface.

Both parties look at each other and then close their eyes.

Bring your attention and focus into the heart-lung area and begin to slow your breath down.

Breathe deeply into your abdominal cavity filling your abdominal cavity with your breath.

As you exhale lightly and slightly draw your abdominal muscles back toward your spinal column.

As you exhale let your exhalation be a little longer than your inhalation.

Continue to slow your breath down.

As you continue to slow your breath down become more aware of your partner.

Feel yourself breathing in and out vertically.

Do this for a cycle of 5-6 times.

Now begin to breath out horizontally toward your partner.

Continue to breath in and out toward your partner.

Be aware of your space and your partner's space.

Allow yourself to get a sense of your space and your partner's space blending and merging.

Be aware of your space separate and distinct and be aware of the space where you and your partner's space is blending and merging.

❧

Open Eye Partner Meditation

This is a wonderful meditation to overcome obstacles in a relationship.

Or, this meditation can be used to instill more intimacy in a relationship.

This meditation also helps one be in the present moment and feel comfortable with oneself as well as with his or her partner.

I have used this meditation with married couples I have worked with as well as many other partnership situations.

Open Eye Partner Meditation

While your eyes are open feel your breath.

Notice how you are breathing.

Consciously slow your breath down.

Breathe deeply into your abdominal cavity.

As you breathe in allow your abdominal cavity to fill with your breath.

As you breathe out slightly and lightly draw your abdominal muscles back toward your spinal column. Continue this rhythm and focus of your breath as you are notice the person in front of you.

Allow your eyes to remain open in a relaxed and unstrained way.

With your head, neck and shoulders relaxed gaze at the person in front of you.

Allow your jaw to open slightly so that the muscles in your mouth, jaw and chin are relaxed.

Continue to slow your breath down.

Notice what you see.

Allow yourself to continue to focus on the person in front of you as you continue to slow your breath down.

Notice any feelings or thoughts that may arise and continue to focus on your partner.

Look completely and with ease at your partner.

Continue breathing deeply and fully allowing the rhythm of your breath to be steady and calm.

Continue this meditation for a period of 5-10 minutes building until you can do easily for any period of time you choose.

Notice how you feel.

Forgiveness Meditation

We meditate in order to be able to see the frailty and the imperma-nence of those who hurt us. Very often those with whom e get most angry are those we most love. -Thich Nhat Hahn

Forgiveness is an act of letting go, of not holding on to the past or what could have been; or what we thought 'should' have been.

One of the types of counseling I facilitate in my practice is bereavement counseling. I have found over the years that if people are allowed to truly grieve, to truly be angry and hurt that the forgiveness process comes naturally. If we allow ourselves to really experience our anger and subse-quently our hurt or fear that we will automatically move on to the new. It is a natural cycle of our survival state. It is not a positive pro-survival pattern to hold on to griev-ances.

However, this does happen if we are stunted in the healing process by judgment or suppression of our emotions and feelings.

If, there are deep psychological wounds this can negatively impact the healing process; however for most individuals this is not the case.

I look at forgiveness as a process of moving on from a role one perceives they were put in or stuck with as well as a process of letting go. As with all processes it takes time.

One muse allow the time to process, heal and naturally move on. The time frame is as different as each individual.

This is also a wonderful meditation is one is feeling stuck in their life. Many times we experience stuck states because we are still holding on to a past experience and are not focused in present time. This has been an extremely powerful meditation for my clients as well as for me on my life path.

So much of what really holds us back is a negative or critical judgment of ourselves and our past actions. We can tend to hold ourselves hostage.

In a way all forgiveness is self forgiveness; which is really just allowing oneself to move on- that is focus on the present and the present choices and situation.

May this meditation bring you peace and free you in ways that you may move forward with ease and realize that all that holds you back is originating as a thought or judgment in your mind.

You may want and need to do this meditation on an ongoing basis.

When we hold on to opinions with aggression, no matter how valid our cause, we are simply adding more aggression to the planet, and violence and pain increase. Cultivating nonaggression is cultivating peace- Pema Chodron

Peace begins with us in self -love and self- acceptance and self -forgiveness. Self – love allows us to let go and move forward. To move from the past into the present is a form of self-acceptance.

If we can't forgive ourselves, move on and let go then how can we forgive others or be open to forgiveness from others?

❧

Forgiveness Meditation

Close your eyes and focus your attention on your heart-lung area.

Simply watch your breath.

Notice each inhalation and each exhalation.

Now, breathe more deeply, begin to breathe into your diaphragm.

Breathe easily into your solar plexus and abdomen.

Now, as you breathe into your solar plexus and abdomen engaging your diaphragm allow your belly to fill with the air of your breath.

Now, as you breathe out slightly and lightly draw your abdominal muscles toward your spinal column.

Continue this pattern of breathing as you focus your inner gaze into your heart -lung area.

Continue to breathe slowly and evenly paced as you focus inward watching your breath.

Slow your breath down as you go deeper within.

As you begin to feel more calm inside think of those you feel have hurt you.

See their name or face in your mind's eye. Sense, see, picture and imagine each individual and how you feel you have been hurt.

Now, with each individual you see inside say their name and in your mind state:

"I now, release you from this role with me".

"I release and I let go"

As you state this words focus on your heart-lung area and picture and imagine your heart pulsing with each inhalation and each exhalation.

As you focus your attention on your heart sense it becoming lighter and lighter opening more and more.

When you feel a sense of completion begin to think of those you feel you have hurt.

See their name or face in your mind's eye. Sense, see, picture and imagine each individual and how you feel you have hurt them.

Now, with each individual you see inside say their name and in your mind state:

"I now release me from this role with you."

"I release and I let go."

As you state these words focus on your heart-lung area and picture and imagine your heart pulsing with each inhalation and each exhalation.

As you focus your attention on your heart sense it becoming lighter and lighter opening more and more.

When you begin to feel a sense of completion begin to think about how you feel you have hurt you.

State in your mind:

"I know release me from this role."

"I release and I let go."

As you state these words focus on your heart-lung area and picture and imagine your heart pulsing with each inhalation and each exhalation.

As you focus your attention on your heart sense it becoming lighter and lighter opening more and more.

Walking Meditation

*Walking mindfully on the Earth can restore our peace and harmony,
and it can restore the Earth's peace and harmony as well.*

*We are children of the Earth. We rely on her for our happiness and
she relies on us also. Whether the Earth is beautiful, fresh and green
or arid and parched depends on our way of walking.*

*When we practice walking meditation beautifully, we massage
the Earth with our feet and plant seeds of joy and
happiness with each step.*

Our mother will heal us and we will heal her."- Thich Nhat Hanh

This meditation is wonderful while on a walk for enjoyment, exercise; or while you are walking to and from completing errands. Or, even while shopping! This is a simple meditation; however the benefits over time are fantastic. I taught this to one of my clients who didn't feel much was changing in his life. He felt stuck in his job situation and personal life. After doing this for a short period of time; he exclaimed " I didn't realize how stuck in my head I was. I noticed so much change in my neighborhood. I don't know why I didn't see all this before."

He felt he had a new lease on life and began to see the positive changes in his personal life. Another client of mine sent me an email after just 2 weeks of doing this meditation stating that she no longer felt depressed.

If we filter everything we do or see by our past experiences and from the frame of mind that "I've already seen this a thousand times before" life can get pretty monotonous.

The truth is our environment, our surroundings, and we are always changing. This meditation also helps one be more in present time.

As you are noticing what is actually around you, you are less focused on your memory of what is around you. Big difference.

Try this for yourself and see.

While walking focus on your breath and begin to slow your breath down.

As you are walking become very aware of how you are breathing and continue to slow your breath down.

The moment you focus on your breath you begin to relax more.

The simple act of focusing on your breath allows your mind to slow down and you experience more calm.

Slow even breath creates a relaxed mind and body.

Notice how you are breathing. And now notice how your breath has changed now that you have a conscious awareness of your breath.

Begin to breath deeper while you continue to consciously slow your breath down.

Now, begin to notice how you are walking.

Feel your pace and your stride, while focused on your breath.

Notice the movement of your legs, your pace, notice your stride.

Feel every movement of your muscles from the large to the small.

Notice how your muscles flex and stretch with your movement.

Now notice where the movement of your body is moving you to.

Notice where you are now.

Notice what is the same around you. Notice what is new.

Notice at least 3 new details around you.

Grounding Meditation

To stay with that shakiness- to stay with the broken heart, with a rumbling stomach, with the feeling of hopelessness and wanting to get revenge- that is the path of true awakening. Sticking with uncertainty, getting the knack of relaxing in the midst of chaos, learning not to panic- this is the spiritual path- Pema Chodron

This is grounding, being grounded. Not to run to hide, to scatter in many directions or create diversion through addictive habits of mind or body.

We may have these feelings and/or visions of running, hiding, screaming, crying. And we may scream or cry and that is ok' however remaining present and there for ourselves with overwhelming and conflicting feelings is grounding.

In certain Native American philosophies to stand is to get understanding. One must stop, observe, look, feel to stand in one place, stand under or in one spot to truly see.

I created this meditation for a client of mine that was going through a cycle of tremendous change. This change had occurred of a span of years with almost no let up and culminated with the crossing over of her spouse. This brought a new set of changing circumstance as well.

When one is in the flux of transition and change one needs to feel grounded or rooted to earth. In other words ones needs to feel a sense of security. And, realistically this security can only come from within.

The truth is all our security comes from *within*. We all need to create a sense of inner completeness, safety and security.

Our security needs to come from us personally first and foremost; then and only then can we attract and receive the true benefits of healthy external emotional support from others. Everything in life changes and everything of the material plane at some point in time declines, erodes, needs to be fixed, or dies.

From our cars, houses, and even our bodies. This subconscious awareness is heighten in times of crisis, transition and change. We can help ourselves wade through the process through breath work and meditation.

❧

Grounding Meditation

This meditation is done standing. (if one cannot, it is perfectly effective to do sitting or lying down)

Stand in a quiet place either indoors or outside in nature.

Stand with your feet shoulder width apart. As you stand slightly bend your legs so that your knees are relaxed and not locked. Relax your pelvic area and slightly tuck your pelvis inward. Relax your head, neck and shoulders. Allow your shoulders to move downward. Slightly move your neck back to allow alignment of your neck to your spinal column. Make sure your chin is not jutting forward. Relax your arms as allowing them to limply hang at your sides. Relax into your stance.

Close your eyes and focus your attention on your heart-lung area.

Simply watch your breath.

Noticing each inhalation and each exhalation.

Now, breathe more deeply, begin to breathe into your diaphragm.

Breathe easily into your solar plexus and abdomen.

Now, as you breathe into your solar plexus and abdomen engaging your diaphragm allow your belly to fill with the air of your breath.

Now, as you breathe out slightly and lightly draw your abdominal muscles toward your spinal column.

Continue this pattern of breathing as you focus your inner gaze into your heart and lung area.

Continue to breathe slowly and evenly paced as you focus inward watching your breath.

Slow your breath down as you go deeper within.

Bring your focus to the bottom half of your body.

Feel the bottom half of your body planted to the earth or ground.

Focus on your feet. Feel your feet steady on the earth or ground.

Sense or picture and image roots going from your bottom half or your body and feet into the earth or ground.

Sense or picture and imagine a light moving from the top of your head out into the sky connecting you to the source of light or sun.

Feel the bottom half of your body and feet rooted to the earth or ground. Feel your feet steady on the earth or ground.

Transforming Fear into Creativity

Within levels of consciousness, the higher frequencies are extremely powerful, and few people routinely experience them as pure states as they are masked by lower energy fields of anxiety, fear, anger, resentment and so on. The high state that people seek, by whatever means, is in fact the experience field of their own consciousness (Self)
- David R. Hawkins M.D., Ph.D.

We are that which we seek, and a lower state of conscious awareness can be raised to a higher state of awareness and frequency.

You literally have all the tools inside you to assist in your own health and well being. You can reduce your stress, release fear, focus better, and learn to harness your body and mind to facilitate the health and life changes you want. Telling someone to not be fearful or that there is nothing to fear is a bit like telling someone to relax. Until you know how to relax, and even more specifically until you know when you are not relaxed, it is really challenging to relax.

Because of our socialization process in the western world we need to re-learn to relax. The knowingness is inside us. We just need to learn to connect back into this inner knowing and natural function.

The same is with fear. There is a healthy fear. A fear that is a message. A warning that it is best to delay or the fear that is a warning or a "no". This is a gut knowing, a gut response.

What we speak of here is an unnatural by product of our society- "chronic fear". Chronic fear or a chronic or unnatural, unwarranted fear state from prolonged stress, being in an unsafe environment or beliefs needs to be transformed or transmuted for health and well-being.

I am asked over and over "How can you get over what you fear?"

You can transform it into creativity. Fear is a very powerful energy. In fact, it is an energy in motion – An emotion. I have found the best way to harness this energy is to use it positively. You can write, draw, go for a walk, run, or even swim. The main thing is not to dwell on what you fear. Ever notice how what you focus on builds a momentum and becomes all you can think about? It is this way with fear. Feed it and it becomes a fire that burns; ignore it and it becomes the smoke that consumes you. If you do not acknowledge your fears they act upon you through non-definable aches, pains and other types of dis-ease. So, one needs to acknowledge what one is fearing and access if it is an actuality or an *eventuality*. Most of our fears are eventualities or worse case scenarios that never manifest; yet the over thinking can wreck havoc on our body and mind.

I have a 3-minute rule. I use this with many of my clients. I say allow yourself 3 - 30 minutes to mull things over and dwell; and then put the fear away and do something proactive and uplifting for yourself. I also suggest listening to my CD Transforming Fear into Creativity and to do the meditation processing on it. I do this, myself, once a day; sometimes more depending on what new challenge I am experiencing. We all have fear. Fear is natural to a degree and doesn't go away; however it can be a powerful tool if it is harnessed right.

❧

Transforming Fear Into Creativity Meditation

Allow yourself to sit or lie down in a comfortable relaxed position.

Close your eyes.

Focus your inner vision on the heart-lung area of your body and just notice your breath.

Notice how you are breathing.

Notice how you are feeling.

Slow your breath down

If any thoughts come into your mind, focus your inner gaze in the heart-lung area and continue to slow your breath down.

Continue to slow your breath down.

Allow your breath to become more steady and more calm

Now, allow yourself to breathe a little deeper, letting the exhalation be a little longer that the inhalation.

Make sure as you are breathing now more slowly that you are relaxing the muscles in your head, neck and shoulders.

Breathe slowing in a relaxed manner, without tensing your muscles or *trying* to force yourself to breathe deeper.

Now, begin to breathe in for the count of three, lightly hold for a count of three, and breathe out for a count of three.

Breathe in for a count of three, lightly hold for a count of three, and breathe out for a count of three.

And one more time breathe in for a count of three, lightly hold for a count of three, and breathe out for a count of three.

As you are now feeling more relaxed, allow your breath to go into its own natural rhythmic pattern.

Now, picture, imagine, sense, see or feel a 'what if' box in your mind. You can create this what if box in any manner or color you choose. This 'what if' box can expand or contract whatever your need.

So focus on this what if box in your mind. See it or sense it very clearly.

Now, put all your cares, worries, and what ifs in this what if box in your mind. Continue to take all your cares, worries and what if s and put them in your what if box. Continue to do this until all your cares, worries, what ifs are now in your what if box.

Now, take the what if box out of your mind. Take the what if box completely out of your mind. Now move it 2- 3 inches away from your mind. Now move it 3- 6 ft. away from your mind.

So you can see it clearly outside of your mind.

You have now moved all your cares, worries and what ifs out of your mind. All your cares, worries and what ifs are safe inside your what if box out of your mind in a place and space where they will be taken care of out of your mind.

Now, that all your cares, worries and what ifs are out of your mind there is more space and light inside.

Now begin to focus on how you want to feel. As you create the feeling that you now want to feel move that feeling into the space in your mind. Now feel the space in your mind with more peace and calm; so that there is now more and more peace and calm inside your mind.

Subtle Energy Meditation

If we are beings of energy then it follows that we can be affected by energy. As unbelievable as it might seem this higher dimensional energy is predicted by Einstein's famous equation, E=Mc2.
— Richard Gerber M.D.

This meditation greatly enhances the awareness of the energy that we are comprised of and that is present all around us.

This is the pranic life force energy of all of life. This is the life force energy that is life and animates all of life.

This energy animates all living beings and life itself.

This energy is life, without this energy there is no life.

❧
Subtle Energy Meditation

Allow yourself to sit or lie down in a comfortable relaxed position.

Close your eyes.

Focus your inner vision on the heart-lung area of your body and just notice your breath.

Notice how you are breathing.

Notice how you are feeling.

Slow your breath down

If any thoughts come into your mind, focus your inner gaze in the heart-lung area and continue to slow your breath down.

Continue to slow your breath down.

Allow your breath to become more steady and more calm

Now, allow yourself to breathe a little deeper, letting the exhalation be a little longer that the inhalation.

As you continue to slow your breath down relax the muscles in your head, neck and shoulders.

Now, begin to breathe in for the count of three, lightly hold for a count of three, and breathe out for a count of three.

Breathe in for a count of three, lightly hold for a count of three, and breathe out for a count of three.

And one more time breathe in for a count of three, lightly hold for a count of three, and breathe out for a count of three.

As you are now feeling more relaxed, allow your breath to go into its own natural rhythmic pattern. Notice how you are breathing.

Bring your attention into your heart-lung area and focus on the space and place in between your inhalation and exhalation. There is a space in between the in breath and the out breath focus on that place inside. Now, go a little deeper inside and focus within.

Bring your attention and focus to the back of your body. Be aware of the back of your body.

Now focus your attention 2-3 inches behind you.

Become aware of the energy at the back of your body.

Focus your attention 1 ft. behind the back of your body.

Now, focus your attention and awareness 3 ft.

As you continue to slow your breath down focus your attention and awareness 6-8 ft. behind you.

Continue focusing your awareness as far behind you as you want to.

Now, bring your attention and focus to the bottom half your body.

Feel your feet.

Now, expand your attention and focus 2-3 inches beyond your feet.

Now, 1 ft. 3 ft, 6-8 ft below you.

Feel your awareness going deep into the earth as far as you can.

Now, bring your attention and focus to left side of your body and feel the energy of this side of your body.

Continue this awareness process as far as you want to..

Then bring your attention and focus to the right side of your body and feel the energy of this side of your body. Continue this awareness process as far as you want to..

Now, bring your attention and focus to the front of your body and feel the front of your body.

Notice how you are breathing. Notice the rhythm and pattern of your breath. Be aware of your heart beating.

Now, focus your attention and focus 2-3 inches in front of your body.

Now, expand your attention and focus out in front of your body as far as you need or want to.

Bring your attention and focus to the top of your head and feel the energy at the top of your head.

Expand your attention and focus 2-3 inches beyond the top of your head.

Expand your attention and focus 3ft beyond the top of your head.

Claiming Your Space Meditation

So how is the mind- the mind being all the senses, the emotions, the memories, the prejudices, the principles, the ideals, experiences, the totality of that, which is the psyche, which is the me- how is that to end and yet act in this world? Is that possible?- Krishnamurti

We need our little mind, our local mind as it is sometimes called. It is the "me" that Krishnamurti talks about. However, this me can feel insecure, afraid or swallowed up with the whole of life.

In spiritual development and integration we learn to balance the me with the I Am That- the collective. We learn to balance a new set of boundaries and in this balancing therein lies a deep inner peace, sense of joy and inner security.

A joy and inner security from the inside out. Claiming your space reaffirms your right to be, to be here on this earth living your life authentically.

This right to be starts with a knowing and then a feeling and then you live it knowing it is so.

CB

Claiming Your Space Meditation Process

Close your eyes.

Allow your body to get into a comfortable relaxed position.

Now begin to consciously slow your breath down. Let your out breath be a little bit longer than your in breath; almost like an inward and subtle sigh. Perhaps sit a little straighter. Just straighten your body so that you are more upright and notice how you feel. Notice any subtle or obvious changes in your breath or how you are feeling.

Now relax your shoulders, allow your chin to slightly drop in towards your chest. This opens up the back of your neck and stretches your spine. Do this with ease, no force is needed. You need not touch your chin to your chest, just a natural relaxing of your head, neck and shoulders. Make sure your jaw is relaxed and breath with your mouth in a relaxed position . Breathe through your nose slowly and calmly. Continue to slow your breath down.

Close your eyes and focus your attention on your heart-lung area.

Simply watch your breath.

Noticing each inhalation and each e x halation.

Now, breathe more deeply, begin to breathe into your diaphragm.

Breathe easily into your solar plexus and abdomen.

Now, as you breathe into your solar plexus and abdomen engaging your diaphragm allow your belly to fill with the air of your breath.

You will feel a slight ballooning sensation. Allow this with comfort and ease.

Now, as you breathe out slightly and lightly draw your abdominal muscles toward your spinal column.

Continue this pattern of breathing as you focus your inner gaze into your heart and lung area.

Continue to breathe slowly and evenly paced as you focus inward watching your breath.

Now bring your attention and focus to the top of your head.

Notice how you feel.

Picture and imagine a bucket of light being gently poured over your body and mind.

Receive this light and feel this light going through you and around you.

Now, picture, imagine, sense, see, or feel this light going down the right side of your body, the left side of your body, the back of your body, the front of your body.

Now, picture, imagine, sense, see, or feel this light at the bottom half of your body and at the top of your body.

As you exhale see this light expanding out and around you 360 degrees 3 ft. around you.

Now, as you breath in feel this light coming into you.

And, as you breath out feel this light radiating out around you 3 ft., 6 ft, and even 12 ft.

Feel yourself in this bubble calm, centered, and focused inside.

In your mind state to yourself:

This is my own sacred, safe space within and without.

I am safe. I am secure.

No comes in unless I need or want them to.

Feel yourself safe and calm.

Mantra- Sacred Sound as a Meditation Path

I once heard this phrase:
If "It" is all illusion anyway, might as well pick an empowering one.

Many people have a mantra, a repetitive saying or phrase going round and round in their mind. The problem is it usually isn't an empowering one!

Mantras are intended to deliver the mind from illusion. The mantras or sacred words are to affirm and confirm our spiritual truth.

Modern science has confirmed what yogis, healers and mystics have known for thousands of years - that *sound* is able to effect the chemistry of the body and mind, and alter thought patterns. Sound is a wavelength that travels through space and time. This vibration effects us. We not only hear sound we can feel it, and therefore it resonates in our body. Mantras are thought to be "thought forms " in sound.

They can bring peace, calm, relaxation and a sense of inner joy.

It may sounds like a weird New-Agey concept when you first hear about Mantra Meditation.

Mantra Meditation is a VERY Powerful technique! And, it is just that another technique another way of accessing to your inner state and the power and presence within.

You will discover that the repetition of Mantra allows your mind to focus and concentrate more completely on sound, and clear away other thoughts, emotions and distractions which divert our energies. Our senses become more acute and our mind become sharper and more perceptive as the mind clears away the jumble of unnecessary inner dialogue. We learn to preserve the our mental, and emotional energies. This enables us to develop a direction and focus in our actions. We become drawn to an uncomplicated and non-competitive life, and we transform our previous attitudes about work into a new-found appreciation in simple aspects of life. In our daily external actions, we are physically active and capable. Internally, we maintain a condition of perpetual meditation. Our simplest labors become an offering, a meditation in and of themselves.

What is it? Mantra Meditation is the technique of using sound, words and unifying phrases to still the reactive mind and open the heart to more love and fulfillment.

The reactive mind is the part of the mind that reacts to every bit of stimuli it receives or sees. This part of the mind is also described as the "monkey mind" the mind like a monkey jumps and jumps around. The "monkey mind" (no offense to monkeys ☺) jumps between dual thinking. "I want this, no I want that." "This is good, this is bad." The dual mind is always swinging back and forth.

The mantra gives the mind something to do, something to ponder.

When you are using mantra you are using your mind to go beyond your mind to oneness.

Mantra is a Meditation Technique of Devotion or Bhakti as it is called in Sanskrit is a deeply spiritual and sacred practice for many meditators, but you do not need to be "a religious" person to experience the gifts Mantra Meditation has to offer.

Mantras can be songs as in chanting or Kirtan as it is called in Sanskrit. Kirtan is the gathering together with others to chant either by singing the mantra or call and response.

In call and response a core group will begin the chant (the call) and the remaining larger group will respond by singing or saying the chant the core group chanted.

Mantras as sounds or words can be whatever you choose - they do not need to be Sanskrit Mantras (Sanskrit is an Ancient Language of India, used frequently in Yoga).

A Mantra can be sound, word or phrase repeated over and over until it integrates into your consciousness - frees the mind from its constant thinking, and elevates you to an expanded state of awareness of peace and calm.

In this state, you can connect with your soul at its most profound level, achieving a state of universal consciousness.

You can use whatever sounds you like. During an inhalation you may say "Breathing in peace and during your exhalation "Breathing out stress". You may say simply say "Om"- the universal sound of oneness and expanded consciousness.

A mantra can be an affirmation stated over and over in your mind.

"I am peace." "I am calm."

A fake it till you make it approach sometimes works. ☺

Mantra is often taught using Sanskrit words or phrases. The Sanskrit mantras are based on sacred sounds that have been around for thousands of years and some say encoded in our dna and collective unconsciousness. For this reason you really don't mean to know the meaning of a mantra on an intellectual level, but to feel the meaning in your heart. This transforms you and brings you into the oneness of the All That Is. This brings peace and calm into your life. Mantras like other forms of meditation have been shown to lower blood pressure and aid in other matters of health and wellness.

Some common Mantras are listed below:

OM - the sound of the Universe (vibration of all living things)

Sat Nam – Truth- I Am Truth

So Ham Ham So- I Am That- That I Am

Om Namah Shivaya - I bow to the God, All That Is; Presence within you that is You. I honor you. I respect you

Shanti, Shanti, Shanti - Peace, peace, peace

There are mantra chants in English. In fact the spiritual group Self Realization Fellowship chant and sing in English. For Sanskrit chants you can check out Siddha Yoga and the Golden Bridge in California for chanting in Punjabi, the language of the Sikhs, that is a variant of Hindi with some Persian influence. There are many forms of chanting, spoken word, singing or prayer in all languages.

In this little book I won't cover them all. However I hope I have opened a window into this aspect of meditation and piqued your interest.

⋈
The Eternal Om

Om is a sanskrit word (mantra, which means sacred word or sound) that means basically the contemplation of the reality of All That Is. It is a contemplating of the 'glue' that holds all of life together, is life and comprises life. It is the energy of all life forms and life itself. It is said when one says the word om on feels a deep and infinite connection to the All That Is of all life. It is also said that the word/sound om is the sound of the universe and the hum of earth.

This meditation is very calming and sends a tingly and vibrating feeling throughout the body.

A client of mine who is a professional dancer swears by this meditation for calming her nerves and energizing her.

Allow yourself to sit or lie down in a comfortable relaxed position.

Close your eyes.

Focus your inner vision on the heart-lung area of your body and just notice your breath.

Notice how you are breathing.

Notice how you are feeling.

Allow yourself to breathe a little deeper, letting the exhalation be a little longer that the inhalation.

Make sure as you are breathing now more slowly that you are relaxing the muscles in your head, neck and shoulders.

Breathe slowing in a relaxed manner, without tensing your muscles or *trying* to force yourself to breathe deeper.

Now, allow your chin to slightly drop in towards your chest. This opens up the back of your neck and stretches your spine. Do this with ease, no force is needed. You need not touch your chin to your chest, just a natural relaxing of your head, neck and shoulders. Make sure your jaw is relaxed and breath with your mouth in a relaxed position . Breathe through your nose slowly and calmly. Continue to slow your breath down.

Close your eyes and focus your attention on your heart-lung area.

Simply watch your breath.

Noticing each inhalation and each e x halation.

Now, breathe more deeply, begin to breathe into your diaphragm.

Breathe easily into your solar plexus and abdomen.

Now, as you breathe into your solar plexus and abdomen engaging your diaphragm allow your belly to fill with the air of your breath.

You will feel a slight ballooning sensation. Allow this with comfort and ease.

Now, as you breathe out slightly and lightly draw your abdominal muscles toward your spinal column.

Continue this pattern of breathing as you focus your inner gaze into your heart and lung area.

Continue to breathe slowly and evenly paced as you focus inward watching your breath.

Now that you are more aligned with your breath each time you breathe out say the word om. So that as you exhale you are quietly and softly saying the word om deep into your solar plexus and abdominal cavity. As you are quietly saying the word om lightly and easily draw your abdominal muscles toward your spinal column. When all your breath is out from your exhalation breathe in deeply allowing your abdominal cavity to fill with your breath of life.

Allow the the word om to reverberate along the middle of your body.

So Ham – Ham So Mantra

Literal meaning in Sanskrit- I Am That- That I am

This is a great mantra to relieve stress. With the use of this sacred mantra you begin to feel your connectedness to All That Is and all of life. You can begin to feel at oneness, and feel more safety, peace and calm in the world. It is said that this mantra erases the illusion of separation.

Of course when we feel connected, safe and calm in the world we will experience less stress in our everyday living.

You can chant this in Sanskrit or English.

In Sanskrit you would breath in and as you breath in say:

"So Ham" "Ham So"

In English you would simply say: I Am That That I Am

As with all mantras you breathe in and mentally say the mantra, visualize the mantra, and hear the mantra in your mind with each breath. You can also speak this mantra outloud.

Breathing in say So Ham Ham So

Do this for 10 or 15 minutes. Or, to really deepen your practice keep repeating this internally throughout your day.

I invite you to create your own sacred mantra. What empowering words are sacred to you? What sounds? What music? You can also combine with movement to create sacred movement. What rhythm soothes your soul and calms your mind? Is it swaying, jogging, dancing?

Try mantra meditation while you jog or spin. Perhaps while walking or driving. You can make your meditation practice more relevant to you and therefore more sacred by creating your own meditations and breath awareness.

Awareness of States of Being Meditation

Within our "tuned", resonant and holographic matrix of experience, the ability to alter energy within any level, produces an effect that is felt through the whole remainder of the system. Subtle as they appear, our feelings and intentions are your primary tools t shift the energy of creation in general and specifically, within your creations.
- Gregg Braden

This is an excellent meditation for positively training the mind not to attach to every thought or feeling. The mind thinks and the body feels. These are main functions of the body-mind.

Yet, people think or feel that they 'have' to follow every feeling or thought; and sometimes pay too much attention to what is just a thought and not actual reality.

It is important to honor our feelings and listen to them. However an important component to knowing which feelings are messages of intuition is to be able to observe our thoughts and feelings to gain a certain level of objectivity and neutrality.

I have used this meditation with many of my clients. I have use it also with many stress reduction or post traumatic stress patients that have been referred to me from medical doctors or psychiatrists.

One of the leading causes of stress are 'worry thoughts' or what is called 'circular thinking'- thoughts that go round and round.

If one can learn to allow the thoughts to go round and round; and yet redirect the focus of the mind peace and calm ensue reducing stress.

If one feeds the thoughts by following the thoughts an endless loop is set in the mind and one literally get entangled in the web…And it all starts with one thought or word.

If you have the same reoccurring thoughts and feelings you may even want to write them down on a sheet of paper or in a journal.

You want to access if the thoughts or feelings are indicating an immediate need or concern. Most of these; in fact an overwhelming percentage do not. These meditation is to assist you in not allowing your thoughts to run away with you putting you at the effect of them.

The awareness of states of being meditation teaches one to not suppress thoughts or emotions; which would definitely be unhealthy; but to train the mind to not focus on the negative thought patterns that created negative and stressful feelings.

If you focus on your breath your mind will follow. And, as you focus on your breath you create more peace and relaxation inside.

❧
Awareness of States of Being Meditation

Close your eyes.

Notice what you are thinking and feeling.

Allow your thought to be there in your mind.

Allow your feelings to be in your body.

Bring your attention and focus to your heart-lung area.

Allow your body to get into a comfortable relaxed position.

Now begin to consciously slow your breath down. Let your out breath be a little bit longer than your in breath; almost like an inward and subtle sigh. Perhaps sit a little straighter. Just straighten your body so that you are more upright and notice how you feel. Notice any subtle or obvious changes in your breath or how you are feeling.

Now relax your shoulders, allow your head, neck and shoulders to relax more. Make sure your jaw is relaxed and breathe with your mouth in a relaxed position . Breathe through your nose slowly and calmly. Continue to slow your breath down.

As you notice the thoughts that your mind is thinking simply say 'thinking' mentally in your mind.

As you notice any feeling your body is feeling simply say 'feeling' mentally in your mind.

Notice the thoughts you are thinking and simply label them as thinking and bring your attention and focus back to your breath.

Notice any feelings your body is feeling and simply label them thinking and bring your attention and focus back to your breath.

Each and every time a thought comes into your mind simply bring your attention and focus back to your breath.

Simply watch your breath keeping your attention and focus on your breath.

Noticing each inhalation and each exhalation.

Now, breathe more deeply, begin to breathe into your diaphragm.

Breathe easily into your solar plexus and abdomen.

Now, as you breathe into your solar plexus and abdomen engaging your diaphragm allow your belly to fill with the air of your breath.

You will feel a slight ballooning sensation.

Allow this with comfort and ease.

Now, as you breathe out slightly and lightly draw your abdominal muscles toward your spinal column.

Continue this pattern of breathing as you focus your inner gaze into your heart and lung area.

Continue to breathe slowly and evenly paced as you focus inward watching your breath.

Allow yourself to bring your attention and focus back to your heart-lung area and focus on your breath.

Without judgment on what you are thinking simply label your thoughts as thinking and bring your attention and focus back to your breath and continue to slow your breath down.

Without judgment on what you are feeling simply label your feelings as feeling and bring your attention and focus back to your breath and continue to slow your breath down.

Releasing Pain

The first noble truth of the Buddha is that when we feel suffering it doesn't mean that something is wrong. What a relief. Finally somebody told the truth. Suffering is part of life and we don't have to feel that it's happening because we personally made a wrong move.
— Pema Chodron

We do go through tough times in our life and sometimes through physical challenges, disease or other conditions we do experience pain. We can learn to manage or even alleviate this in some cases, in fact many. I think one o the most important focuses to healing is to come to an inner place of non – judgment. Take care of yourself like you would a good friend or loved one.

Our mind can and does affect our body. There has been a lot of research in this area; especially in the arena of body-mind therapy as well as psychoimmuniology.

I feel though we can create a better relationship with our body through awareness and gentleness. It is not enough to 'will' the body to do what we need or want it to do. Just like any good relationship it takes time to build trust and rapport. Consistency definitely helps in this process. So as you build a rapport with your body-mind you can create a more peaceful inner environment for yourself, even during time of pain and discomfort.

This meditation has been used for back pain, migraines, post surgery healing and many other healing processes.

I have seen one client of mine use it for a phoebia of heights.

At one point a client of mine even used this to completely alleviate a head cold he had while on vacation.

The head cold completely disappeared and he was able to enjoy the remainder of his vacation as well as climb the pyramids that he could not climb originally because of his head cold.

C3

Pain Management Meditation Process

Picture, imagine, sense or feel yourself in your own bubble of light. You are in your own bubble of light with a shield of protection, calm inside.

And now notice that this bubble of light or circle of light encircles and enfolds you. You are calm inside.

This circle of light that encircles and enfolds you is your sphere of life, your sphere of influence. This circle of light that encircles you is you circle of life experience. Anything that you no longer need or want to experience just move it out of your circle of light. Any situation, feeling, emotion, person or state of being you no longer want or need to experience just move it outside of your circle of light, off and away.

And so picture or image that thought or feeling you no longer want as an object or a shape. Make that feeling a shape. Good. And now when that shape becomes bigger the feeling or thought becomes bigger. So make it smaller now, make it much smaller now. And as it is smaller it begins to fade away. And, so now that it is much smaller just move it out of your circle of light. Move out off and away. Move 3" outside your circle of light now 6" and now 12" and now 3" , 6' now 12' and now outside of the room, the building and so far that you no longer see this shape. It is gone, faded away, gone.

Creating Sacred Space

We all need a place to go to refresh and rejuvenate.

A place that is all our own that we feel comfortable and at peace.

Perhaps, for some it is a place to unwind…But it is nonetheless an actual place; a physical place.

We can create this internally and mentally; and this is a major goal in meditation. However, the external tends to mirror the internal and the internal tends to mirror the external. A calm and orderly person usually lives in a calm and orderly environment. Cleaning out one's closet or clearing clutter off one's desk creates a feeling of accomplishment and relief. Our environment definitely affects and reflects our inner mental state. A truly peaceful environment people can feel. The people who live and work in a peaceful environment have this inner peace within. This cannot be fabricated. One can feel peace whether in a person or in an environment. It is a very real and tangible feeling or perception.

To create this peace within we have to have a place to build the structure that creates the fabric of our inner peace. This structure has a few components. One is the very act of 'practicing' meditation daily, another part is using meditation as an actual 'tool' to create the state of mind you want to experience; and a very integral part is the act of creating a meditative environment that one uses on a consistent basis.

The key word here is consistent. If we don't practice consistently, then we can't build a foundation of inner peace.

It is equally important that we have a place in our home and perhaps even at our office that represents peace of mind.

One has to have a specific space that triggers consciously and subconsciously the attitude that one is going to need to perform a certain activity.

It is similar with many activities not just meditation.

A painter, a musician, a dancer, a lawyer, an actor, a professor has a specific place or space to go and practice their craft or skill. A student who has homework to do has a better chance of productivity and retaining the information without external distraction. An accountant has a specific place. A trader, stockbroker, or writer has a specific place. A chef or cook has his or her kitchen.

When we go to the gym or health club to work out the very act of putting on our gym clothes and driving to the club begins to focus our mind to prepare for the activity at hand. Driving to the office to start the work day, sitting at our computer at our home office, or even walking to school all act as triggers to create the state of mind we will need to focus on what we are about to do.

Years ago I studied dance and did some performance. I began to see a direct connection between the practicing of the techniques of dance and performing. If one practiced well, one tended to perform better. Technique disappeared and the dance and the dancer became one. This is the same with meditation. Practicing daily one then takes this technique out into their world. One another note, one day one of my dance instructors shared an observation in class to illustrate the psychology of dance. She stated that a true dancer would come to class and slowly enter the studio, purvey the room and pick a spot at the dance bar that she/he felt most comfortable. This was so true. In fact, this occurs in dance classes, aerobic classes, yoga classes, and most types of classes or group settings. We all need a space that supports and enhances the mindset we need to do a particular activity. And, this place no matter the location needs to be and tends to be consistent.

This being said I think you can see the correlation with these activities and the activity of meditation. You will have a much greater chance of developing the kind of mind that can access peaceful states of being at will if you practice consistently and in a consistent place.

In creating your sacred space I suggest you pick a place in your home to start with and create an environment that reminds you of the peace and calm you want to experience daily. This will be a special place where you go to meditate and focus on you. This sacred space is a place that you honor and nurture you. This space can be a specific room or a certain space in a room. It is very important that even if the space is an area of 2ft.by 2ft that it only be for you and this specific purpose. It is your sacred, safe and special space. This place is a place to remind you of your inner connection and your connection to the interrelation of All That Is. This is a place to relax and rejuvenate your spirit. You may also want to personalize this room or space in a way that puts you in touch with your spiritual nature.

One of my clients created a room with a mural on the wall with scenery from her favorite vacation places. She had a mountain scene, a meadow and a beach scene all on one large expanse of wall. She also, outfitted her sacred space with a water fountain, a shelf with special objects and beach rocks. Another client decorated a space in his dining room with a mandala (sacred art piece) on the wall and a simple cushion to sit on for meditation. One of my clients has a reading and meditation corner. This particular client travels a lot and carries a travel meditation set comprised of items that remind her of her spiritual nature, reinforce a state of calm and give her assurance. .At one point, one of my clients complained she didn't have the time or space as her house was small and she had a husband and three small children that all needed her attention throughout the day and night. The only extra room was her husband's office and he used that nightly. I coached her and suggested she surely could find some small space to make her own. She did. She created a space in the bedroom. She rearranged the furniture in the bedroom, made more space on her side of the bed and created her 'special corner'. She then made a sign on the computer that said 'mom's time' and had it laminated and when she needed her quiet time or meditation time she put the sign on the door and did her meditation practice.

Sometimes we don't have a lot of time or space, but we can alter our consciousness in a short span of time.

A mini mental vacation can be a way of creating sacred space.

It is a good idea to take a little breather for yourself when you feel the need. This taking time for oneself is an act of self love and respect. It gives our life meaning and honors the sacredness of who we are and how far we have traveled on the road of life. Many of us take time for a friend, spouse, lover or family member in need. It is seen as a way of showing care, concern and being in touch. Well, we need this for ourselves also.

I like to take a mini mental vacation when I am feeling a bit overwhelmed with the projects I have.

I have a sound loop of a digital image I took of a creek in Mammoth, California on holiday. The sound loop is a continuous play of the sound of the creek. I also made the image into a desktop picture for my computer. You can use as sound loop or any image that reminds you of relaxation or peace.

Whenever I feel as if I could use a bit of nature to align to my own true nature I turn on the sound loop of the flowing water of the creek and keep my full awareness on the sound of the water flowing as well as looking at the picture of the beautiful green reeds and image of the water flowing through the rocks rhythmically As I focus on the rhythm of the water flowing I begin to slow my breath down.

I keep this process up of slowing my breath down as well as taking in the sounds of the water flowing and the sight of the creek in picture form on my computer screen.

I don't have to go anywhere, be anywhere; but right here right now.

I can use my knowledge of the breath of life and allow my mind to rest in my true nature. I can even close my eyes and I am right there with all the sights and sensations of the atmosphere of this creek.

This is a mini vacation, and well worth it. We are all worth taking the time to just reflect, feel and honor where we are in the present moment of time.

Take this time to refresh and renew. You can afford this 10 minutes just for you.

We all can spare a few minutes a day to ourselves and many of us even more.

I suggest you create your own version of this kind of meditation. It can be visual, auditory with music and sound; or kinesthetic, with mala or rosary beads or even a rock you hold. Or, perhaps you sit on a cushy pillow, sit or walk on the beach or sit on a grassy patch. You can even bring in the olfactory by burning incense or spraying an essential oil spray of lavender to relax or citrus to re-energize. The more of your senses you can bring in the better for your experience of peace and calm. You will find what triggers peace and calm in you and brings in more inspiration and refreshment into your mini vacation.

If you are short on time and long on stress. This meditation is great for recharging the "inner" batteries or connecting in with a relaxed state for creative solutions.

The more energy and dedication you can put into your practice the more you will feel the effects of your practice. In a sense you are communicating to yourself and those around you that this is an important aspect of your life. You greatly enhance your sense of self and self esteem by designating a time to celebrate the sacredness of your being and life path. If you take the time to know, honor and respect yourself you will begin to attract people that honor and respect you. You needn't do anything in particular other than be you. And, really isn't this all meditation is, being yourself.

This is what the practice of meditation does. It allows you to discover you, acknowledge you, the authentic you - the true you. The you beyond what you do for a living, the type of car you drive, where you live, who you know, and how your body looks or feels, This you is beyond what you have or don't have. This you is your inner you. This you; recognizes the truth of who you are.

A spiritual being experiencing and expressing life.

Taking the time to be in your sacred space is an act that honors, nurtures, validates and reinforce the positive in your life. As you create this sacred space in your home it permeates throughout your life. The sacred space that is represented in a special place in your home begins to radiate through your attitude, demeanor, and self-perception.

When you see yourself and your life path as sacred you love and accept yourself unconditionally and this love and acceptance is reflected back to you through your relationships and life experiences.

I honor you and your path, and wish you much peace so that you may create sacred space in your everyday living.

Your Next Step - A Contemplative Meditation

Now that you have read the book and have familiarized yourself with some of the meditations and meditation processes here it is time for a bit of a personal check in. It is important at various stages and parts of our path to contemplate where we have been, and acknowledge and validate how far we have come and what we know now.

This contemplation and acknowledgment builds our spiritual strength, reinforces us emotionally and mentally as well builds a confidence in our inner knowing.

On some level meditation is about trusting our inner knowing, our inner wisdom and our Divine path unfolding.

Through the practice of meditation we learn to live more and more in a meditative state. And, perhaps even more importantly we learn how to connect in and allow or access this state when we need to or find that we have moved out of our center.

So take some time to get into a relaxed meditative state and do the following contemplative meditation: (it is helpful to write your answers in a journal to reflect back)

What have you learned, come away with? And how can you integrate this into your everyday living?

How can you use the tool or technique of meditation to live more and more in a meditative state throughout your day?

What seems to trigger stress for you and which meditations or breathwork are helpful to you in getting back to your center and a more meditative state?

What insights do you have about your spiritual path and meditation practice?

What new insight, awareness and way of being do you have since integrating more meditation into your life?

Is there some adjustment to your meditation practice to make it benefit you more?

Do you need more time to meditate?

Do you need to use the tool of meditation more consistently?

What are the uses of meditation that most benefit you?

Where do you need and want to visit & check out (Sacred Sites, Meditation Groups, etc)?

What is the next step for you to integrate into your meditation/spiritual practice and life path?

5 Minute Meditations for the
5 Minute Meditator

By now you know your breath is a wonderful tool for relaxation and it is free. It is said that when the breath is steady the mind is calm. The next time you are feeling rushed or stressed over some situation try these exercises; better yet, pick one and try it for 30 days and notice how you change your overall attitude in life.

These meditations are to integrate into your life when you need a quick little boost or alignment.

Time is a consideration, arbitrary at best, and some say an illusion.

You can get to a point in your mediation practice that it doesn't take hours to get into a centered and relaxed state.

You can now be your own stress management consultant. You can assist yourself and others in visualizing goals. If your day gets hectic at least you will be relaxed and centered inside.

Whether a quick goal setting meditation or a meditation to center or reduce stress you can learn to attune more and more quickly to a meditative state.

With practice you can learn to attune in minutes or just with the thought of calm and centered – There you are.

❧

The 5-Minute Centering Process

Ever notice how hard it is to get out of a bad mood? It is easier to get out of a bad mood by not getting into one! How you might say? You can set the tone for your day at the beginning of the day.

Your day literally starts before you get out of your bed.

Start your day by not rushing…. Take a little extra time getting out of your bed and do a 3 minute focused meditation.

After awakening don't just rebound out of your bed.

Lie there for a minute or two, close your eyes.

Focus on your breathing and slow your breath down.

Tell yourself "I am in the flow of my day. I am calm and centered inside."

Now bring your attention and focus to the top of your head and notice how you are breathing.

Begin to notice the part of you that is observing you.

If thoughts come in your mind that's ok, focus on your breath and keep it at a slow stead pace.

Repeat to yourself "I am in the flow of my day. I am calm and centered inside."

Feel what this flow can feel like and say

"I am calm and centered inside." "I am calm and centered inside."

ରେ

The 5-Minute Stress Buster

Take about 5 minutes for yourself, go somewhere where you can have some quite time. Now get in a comfortable relaxed position.

Or, you can do this at your desk, even standing in a line at a store.

Allow yourself to take this time to focus on relaxation and rejuvenation. Close your eyes. Now with your inner gaze focus on the heart – lung area of your body and begin to slow your breath down.

Allow your breath to slow down. Now begin to breathe in for a count of 3, lightly hold for a count of 3, and exhale slowly all the way out for a count of 3.

Allow yourself to breathe all the way into your stomach-abdomen area.

Do these 5 or 6 times. Now allow your breath to go back to its natural rhythm and simply watch your breath.

Notice how you feel.

Focus on each inhalation and each exhalation.

Let your exhalation be a little longer than your inhalation.

If any thoughts come in your mind, simply label them as "thinking" and bring your focus back to your breath.

If any feelings come in your body label them as "feeling" and bring your attention and focus back to your breath.

You can even say "thinking" and "feeling in your mind" with each thought or feeling that comes up.

Continue to notice your breath. Continue to slow your breath down. Continue to bring your conscious awareness back to your breath.

If any thoughts come in your mind, simply label them as "thinking" and bring your focus back to your breath.

If any feelings come in your body label them as "feeling" and bring your attention and focus back to your breath.

Continue with this until you are more and more focused on your breath and/or you lose track of your inner dialogue and are just peacefully centered inside.

Now see how much more calm and relaxed you are.

You can now decide to live in a relaxed and healthy way, and, like anything else practice makes perfect.

ଔ
The 5-Minute Visionary

Dreams belong to us. They become for us the bearers of the new possibility, the enlarged horizon… giving to our days the magic of the stars. - Howard Thurman

To me this enlarged horizon is our vision. Through meditation and living in the meditative state more and more it is possible to expand our belief in what is possible.

The meditative state expands our vision.

You can be your own life coach by visualizing and rehearsing your success twice a day. You can be your own inspiration by tapping into the power and presence within.

It is said if you can see it, feel it, you can be it.

In changing our thoughts we change our life.

When you do this visioning exercise connecting to the *feeling tone* of the vision and goal is key. The feeling tone is the feeling beyond the emotion of the goal.

Frequency is also key here. The more you can see it and feel it the more real it becomes in your mind. This sets up an expectation that creates a result in alignment with the expectation.

You don't need to "worry" or concern yourself with the "how" of the goal. Just continue to focus and align to the goal/s and how you will feel in achieving this goal/s.

You can do it throughout the day and at set intervals.

Research has shown that most people that succeed in their goals can see themselves achieving their goals and living their dream. This is most noted with athletes, who use the power of visualization and focus to meet their goals. If you can see it, and believe it; you can achieve it.

It is best to do this at a time you have for yourself and this process. First, I would suggest writing down your goal.

Write this down in the present tense as if you were already living your goal or dream. Next, you will need to get into a comfortable and relaxed state. It is much easier to create positive changes in a relaxed state. This state also begins to quiet " The Doubter "part of us all. You know the part that says you can't do this! This meditation process connects you to the "I can do this" part of you. The potential and possibility part. The what is of your concern, the how the arena of the higher mind.

Now, close your eyes and get in a comfortable relaxed state. Slow your breath down.

Breathe in for a count of 3. Hold your breath, lightly for a count of 3.

Exhale all the way out for a count of 3.

Do this for a couple of times until you feel more relaxed; Now, visualize yourself experiencing your goal or dream. Keep doing this until you can really see, it and/or feel it.

Notice how you feel and use this feeling to connect more and more with your goal/dream/desire.

Next imagine yourself achieving your goal and living your dream.

Picture it, see it, feel it.

Continue to do this for 30 days.

10 Easy Ways to Ease Stress

1. Breathe! Many of us breathe shallowly, which means we breathe only into our chest. It is more calming, relaxing and healthy to breathe fully into our abdomen using the diaphragm.

2. During long periods of concentrated activity take frequent breaks.

    When working, writing, studying, typing on the computer, or any other focused activity take a break for at least 1 minute per 1 hour of activity. You can stretch, take in a couple of deep breaths, walk around, get a drink of water, or simply go outside; fresh air is wonderful for the body's circulation. The main point is to allow the body a change of pace and recovery time

3. Exercise and get plenty of fresh air. Exercise is not only good for our body, but also our mind. In exercising our brain produces and activates the hormonal substance endorphins which has a sedating, calming, euphoric effect on body and mind creating a mental state of a natural high and feeling "up with life." Cardiovascular exercise also releases in a healthy positive way pent up tension, frustration and anger. Which can be a natural byproduct of life.... so do something beneficial with it!

4. Balanced diet. Get plenty of green vegetables, and whole grains. These foods act as "stress buffers" cleansing, toning, and balancing the body. Also, if you

are taking vitamin supplements they need to have food present in the body to be of benefit. Vitamins work synergistically with food. Also a balanced diet allows the body to be consistently fueled and nourished.

5. Drink plenty of water; preferably filtered water, or spring water. Research has shown that there is no better liquid for the body.

6. Balanced lifestyle. Time for leisure, rest and rejuvenation. A balanced lifestyle includes activities to enhance, harmonize, relax, and integrate mentally, emotionally, spiritually, and physically.

7. Have a creative outlet. A hobby; some activity that does not have to generate income. This can be painting, drawing, sewing, fishing, crafts, reading, writing, journal keeping, writing poetry, or perhaps meeting with friends for a philosophical conversation. A hobby can turn into a business, however that is not the main focus. It is enjoyment and creativity in and of itself.

8. Supportive friends, family; an association with like-minded individuals. It is important for us all to have someone we can share and talk with on an intimate level. This communication and understanding sometimes comes from family members, however most often it comes from friends and associates that we develop a bond with because of similar interests and life situations.

9. A program or outlet that allows you to grow and expand. Studies have shown in the elderly that those that used their mind beneficially did not usually develop Alzheimer's disease. Keep exploring and enjoying that precious gift called "you"

10. Laughter. Laughter is still the best age-old medicine. In fact, there are many clinics and cancer therapies that include this in their treatment. Laugh at yourself, laugh with others.

A bird is able to fly high because he takes her/himself lightly.

Take an active part in your life. It is an expression of YOU....

References & Resources:

This is by no means a complete list of all my study or all the great books or music that are available. This is a starting point. Add your own. Take what resonates with you, leave what doesn't behind, and spin it in a way that makes it your own sacred practice.

Books

Recovering The Soul- Larry Dossey, M.D.

The Essential Krishnamurti - J. Krishnmurti

Bodymind - Ken Dychtwald

Play of Consciousness - Baba Muktananda

Cutting Through Spiritual Materialism - Chogyam Trungpa

The Gift- Hafiz

Where The Mind Meets The Body - Harris Dienstfrey

Science of Breath- Swami Rama, Rudolph Ballentine, and M.D. Alan Hymes, MD

Flow, The Psychology of Optimal Experience-Mihaly Csikszentmihalyi

Handbook To Higher Consciousness- Ken Keyes, Jr.

The Only Dance There Is - Ram Dass

The Blooming Lotus- Thich Nhat Hanh

The Prophet- Kahlil Gibran

40 Day Mind Fast Soul Feast- Dr. Michael Beckwith

Enthusiasm - Swami Chidvilasananda

Courage, The Joy of Living Dangerously - Osho

Awareness The Key to Living in Balance - Osho

When Things Fall Apart – Pema Chodron

Comfortable With Uncertainty – Pema Chodron

Awakening to Zero Point – Gregg Braden

Light on the Path- Swami Muktananda

The Secret of The Golden Flower – translation and explained by Richard Wilhelm

Transforming Fear Into Creativity Meditation process- Michele Meiché

Understanding Universal Laws and Using The Law of Magnetic Attraction- Michele Meiché

The Crystal Temple of Healing - Michele Meiché

The 5 Step Emotional Clearing Process - Michele Meiché

Meditation for Everyday Living - Michele Meiché

Wherever You Go, There You Are: -Jon KabaZinn

Awakening Healing Energy Through the Tao- Mantak Chia

Original Self- Thomas Moore

Awareness - Anthony De Mello

A Cup of Tea – Osho

Meditate- Swami Muktananda

Intelligence- The Creative Response to Now- Osho

Enthusiasm- Swami Chidvilasananda

A Whole New Mind- Daniel Pink

A Guide To The I Ching - Carol K. Anthony

Music/ Kirtan-Chanting

Aeoliah – Angel Love

PC Daviddoff- Bamboo - Raku

El-Hadra – The Mystik Dance

Anugama – Shamanic Dream - Tantra - The Lightness of Being

Deuter – Himalaya – Wind & Mountain – Buddha Nature

Steve Halpern – Comfort Zone, Sound Healing Chakra Suite

Philip Chapman – Contemplation

Sanctuary –David & Steve Gordon

Carlos Nakai – Canyon Trilogy

Jennifer Berezan - Returning

Scott Fitzgerald & Richard Hooper- Dreamland –

Chinmaya Dunster

Joseph Michael Levry

Jai Uttal

Raphael - Music To Disappear In II

Quiet Heart, Spirit Wind - Richard Warner

Krishna Das

Donna DeLory

Dave Stringer

Temple Bhajan Band

Wah

Disclaimer—just earthly 3rd dimensional due diligence. These meditations, meditation processes or breath work are not intended to replace qualified medical health care. If you have or think you have a condition, which requires medical attention, you should promptly consult, and seek a qualified health care professional or medical doctor. The meditations, meditation processes, and breath work are for educational purposes only.

About the Author

Photograph by Pierre Matthieu

Michele Meiche Ct.H.A. H.H.C. Ph.D.

Michele assists others on their life path as a Spiritual Life Coach, Transcendent Healer & Transpersonal Therapist

Michele's gift is in going beyond the conventional form of seminar lecturing and explanations. Her seminars are interactive with a balance of theory and practical application. Since she is a trained teacher as well as a therapist she is able to relay information in an easily assimilative manner. If you really want to know what meditation, self-hypnosis, transpersonal integration, or spiritual healing are and actually experience it, with Michele's seminars you have that option.

As a natural psychic she has always been in touch spiritually, seeing and feeling what many do not; or if they do have been afraid to admit or haven't had the outlet. Her gift is in being this outlet- a conduit so that others can find their own way, their own light. This is part of what she teaches, is for others to open and access to this part of them to aid in transition, crisis, life changes, and stress reduction and to enhance life.

Her life enhancement coaching focuses on self-development and spiritual integration, meditation and breath work, transcendental healing & transpersonal psychology. Esoterically trained, Michele blends the spiritual & metaphysical with the psychological. She has been in the transpersonal and holistic health field for over 20 years and has been in private practice for 11 years.

Michele facilitates seminars and retreats in the United States and Europe. She is the author of a series of transformational Audio CDs and the creator of the Alpha-Theta process 5 Step Emotional Clearing process™

She is involved in television & media as a TV. And radio expert/host for programs that focus on living a conscious lifestyle.

A strong purpose for Michele is assisting people to live in the meditative state more and more consistently and use this state of being for a more fulfilled life. Michele receives tremendous fulfillment from sharing her life experience, expertise, and teaching useful tools and life skills that promote wellness and enhance a person's life.

Michele is involved community outreach programs as well as enrichment programs for adults and youth. She volunteers her time to at risk youth facilities, libraries, rehabilitation centers, as well as schools.

She loves working with children, having taught school at one point in her vocation. She has worked with preschool, kindergarten, elementary, middle school, as well as high school youth. Michele's 'Meditation for Everyday Living' and 'The Magic of Your Inner You' programs have been delivered to children from toddler age to those in their teens and early twenties.

Michele uses her book 'Meditation for Everyday Living' and Her Pamphlet 'The Magic of Your Inner You' as a teaching tool. One of Michele's dreams is to get her CDs, books and 'From Dreams to Reality' video project into schools, rehabilitation centers, juvenile detention centers and at risk youth facilities to inspire youth to find and believe in their gifts, tap into their inner knowing to create a life of fulfillment. Her belief and experience has been that many times the youth just need to be shown the possibilities to get them thinking differently to actualize their own dreams.

For more information, please visit her web site: www.selfinlight.com.